ONCE IS ENOUGH

Once Is Enough

Miles Smeeton

Foreword by Nevil Shute

**WILLIAM
COLLINS**

William Collins
An imprint of HarperCollinsPublishers
1 London Bridge Street
London SE1 9GF
WilliamCollinsBooks.com

1st Floor, Watermarque Building, Ringsend Road
Dublin 4, Ireland

First published by Rupert Hart-Davis Ltd 1959
Also published by Granada Publishing 1984

This edition published by William Collins in 2013

Copyright © The Cochrane Ecological Institute 1959

Miles Smeeton asserts the moral right to
be identified as the author of this work

A catalogue record for this book
is available from the British Library

ISBN 978-0-00-753510-1

Contents

MAPS

Drawn by K. C. Jordan

DRAWINGS

Drawn by the author

Foreword
By NEVIL SHUTE

Some years ago I had an afternoon to spare in Vancouver, so I went down to the yacht harbour to see what sort of vessels Canadian yachtsmen use. There I found *Tzu Hang* moored alongside a pontoon, slightly weather-beaten, sporting baggywrinkle on her runners, and wearing the red ensign. As I inspected her Miles Smeeton came up from below and invited me on board. That was my first meeting with this remarkable man; I did not meet his more remarkable wife till some time later.

The Smeetons had bought *Tzu Hang* in England a year or so previously and they had sailed her out from England across the Atlantic and through the Panama Canal to Vancouver with their eleven-year-old daughter as the third member of the crew. Before buying this considerable ship they had never sailed a boat or cruised in any yacht. They made one trip in her to Holland and then set out across the Atlantic for the West Indies. Navigation was child's play to them; seamanship they picked up as they went along. With only two adults on board they had to keep watch and watch, but did not seem to find it unduly tiring. They made their landfalls accurately, passed the Panama, reached out a thousand miles into the Pacific before they could lie a course for Vancouver, and they arrived without incident. I asked if they had had any trouble on the way. Miles told me that they had been hove to for three days in the Atlantic; the only trouble that they had in that three days was in keeping their small daughter at her lessons. They made her do three hours school work each morning, all the way.

When I began yacht cruising after the First World War it was regarded as an axiom amongst yachtsmen that a small sailing vessel, properly handled, is safe in any deep-water sea. I think that Claude Worth, the father of modern yachting, may have been partly responsible for this idea, and it may well be true for the waters in which he sailed. A small yacht, we said, will ride easily over and amongst great waves if she is hove to or allowed to drift broadside under bare poles; you have only to watch a seagull riding out a storm upon the water, we said. Perhaps we failed to notice that the seagull spreads its wings now and again to get out of trouble; perhaps we were seldom caught out in winds of force 7 or 8 and much too busy then to observe the habits of seabirds, which probably had too much sense to be there anyway.

From time to time our complacent sense of security was just a little ruffled. Erling Tambs, in *Teddy*, was overwhelmed in some way by the sea when running in the Atlantic; his account was not very clear and it was easy for us to assume that he had been carrying too much sail, had been pooped and broached to. The lesson to us seemed obvious; heave to in good time or lie to a sea-anchor, perhaps by the stern if the ship was suitable. Captain Voss, sailing with two friends in a seven tonner in the China Sea, was turned completely upside down so that the cabin stove broke loose and left its imprint on the deckhead above, on the cabin ceiling. But that was a long way away; all sorts of things happen in China. … Captain Slocum was lost in the Atlantic without trace after

2

sailing single-handed round the world—but anything could have happened to him.

It has been left to Miles Smeeton in this book to tell us in clear and simple language just where the limits of safety lie. We now know with certainty that the seagull parallel was wrong. A small yacht, well found, well equipped, and beautifully handled, can be overwhelmed by the sea when running under bare poles dragging a warp, or when lying sideways to the sea hove to under bare poles. The Smeetons have proved it, twice. Twice these amazing people saved their waterlogged, dismasted ship by their sheer competence and sailed her safely in to port, greatly assisted on the first occasion by John Guzzwell. With equal competence they have now produced this lucid and well-written book to tell us all about it.

At the risk of offending the author I must stress the fact that these are most unusual people, lest more ordinary yachtsmen should be tempted to follow them down towards Cape Horn— 'After all, they proved that one can get away with it, didn't they?' Nobody reading this account can fail to realise how excellently they had prepared, equipped, and provisioned their ship for the long voyage from Australia down in to the Roaring Forties. One can say, perhaps, that she was overmasted for that particular trip. But vessels cannot be rigged solely for going round the Horn; she had also to sail through the doldrums of the Equator on her way back to England. I visited the ship in Melbourne before she sailed; she was rugged and tough and functional to the last degree, as were the people in her.

Quite a number of yachtsmen have now sailed round the world with their wives, for the most part running downwind in the Trades in the lower, more generous latitudes. How many of the wives, I wonder, could take a sextant sight from the desperately unsteady cockpit of a small yacht at sea, work out the position line with the massed figures of the tables dancing before one's eyes, and plot it on the chart? Beryl Smeeton can do this with such accuracy that it was common practice on this yacht for anyone who was unoccupied to take the sight and for anybody else to work out the position line; their competence was equal. What can one say of a woman who, catapulted from the cockpit of a somersaulting ship into the sea and recovered on board with a broken collar-bone and a deep scalp cut, worked manually like a man with her broken bone and did not wash the blood from her hair and forehead for three weeks, judging that injuries left severely alone heal themselves best? What can one say of a woman working as a carpenter to repair the gaping holes in the doghouse while the dismasted ship lurches and slithers in enormous seas, who refuses to nail the boards in place but drills a hole for every wood screw and does the job as properly as a professional carpenter could have done it on dry land? These people are quite unusual, and all yachtsmen reading this book had better realise that fact. More ordinary people would undoubtedly have perished.

They had, I think, one gap in the great cloak of competence that wrapped them round; they thought too little of their engine. In a sailing yacht designed to cruise the oceans the auxiliary motor must always take a second place to the sails and gear, yet if the weight and complication of a motor is to be carried in a ship at all it would be better to have a good one, one that will work under extreme conditions. *Tzu Hang* had a petrol motor with the usual electric ignition; this motor, for the sake of the internal accommodation, as is common in week-end yachts, was buried deep down in the bilges under the doghouse deck in a position where it was practically impossible to start it by hand when immersion had killed the starter batteries. After each disaster when a motor would have been a help to the dismasted ship this motor was a useless nuisance to them; the ship would have been lighter and so safer with it overboard. They could have had a hand-starting diesel mounted up in a position where one could swing upon the handle with both hands, driving the propeller-shaft by belts or chains. Accommodation might have suffered slightly, but the motor would have worked as soon as they had drained the water from the crankcase and refilled with oil. In so functional a vessel as *Tzu Hang* I think the motor was unworthy of the rest of her.

The Smeetons and *Tzu Hang* are back in British waters now; I doubt if they will stay there. A few days ago I got a letter from Miles Smeeton. In part it reads:

> We sailed on the 10th for the Firth of Forth, almost with mechanics and shipwrights still on board. Had two days to Hartlepool where we put in on account of a storm warning—and then off for the Forth and bang into a north-westerly gale. We were hove to for three days but *Tzu Hang* behaved beautifully and kept her decks dry and re-established our confidence.

So they go on their way again across the seas. In this admirably written book they have done a good job for yachting. All yachtsmen should read it and be grateful to the valiant people who have dared to chart the limits of their sport.

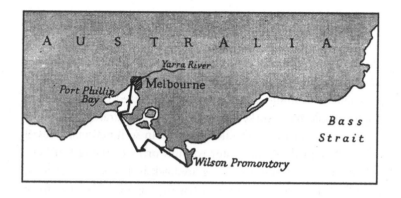

CHAPTER ONE

PREPARATIONS IN MELBOURNE

THE crowd still thronged the Spencer Street bridge when Clio and I came back from the Olympic Games. They were leaning on the parapet and looking at the Royal Yacht, as they had done ever since her arrival in Melbourne. They were in holiday mood, looking for the best angle for their cameras, and full of enthusiasm and pawky Australian humour. Just across the bridge in a shop window a notice had been posted: 'English spik here,' it said; and on the door of the funeral parlour, a little further up the street, there was a card saying briefly that any Olympic visitors were welcome.

Looking down river from the bridge, we could see how it wound its way between wharves, warehouses, and docks, its course marked by high cranes and the masts of ships, until in its last mile it curved between low flat banks to its outlet in Port Philip Bay. In front of us *Britannia*'s beautiful tall bow reached over the bridge, and beyond her, on the other side of the river, an Australian ship was moored. Immediately opposite *Britannia*, and tied up to the south wharf, there was another yacht, also flying the British flag, for she was registered in England, although her home was now in Canada. She was very small compared to her royal neighbour, but she also intended to sail in a few days for England, and by the same route, south of New Zealand and south of Cape Horn. She was called *Tzu Hang*, and she was ours.

Beyond the *Britannia*, and parallel to and across the river from *Tzu Hang*, ran Flinders Street, with its ships' chandlers, whose shops Beryl visited every day with a preoccupied air and carrying long lists in her hand. Behind Flinders Street, the land sloped up to Collins Street, with its banks and clubs and prosperous good-looking buildings, and to the low hills on which the city of Melbourne is built. Not so long ago the river here used to be full of sailing ships, and Clio and I would have seen a forest of masts and spars; but now there were only two, *Tzu Hang* and a big yacht down from Sydney, which was tied up in front of us.

'Look at that idiot cat. She isn't half giving those sails a go,' someone said, calling the attention of his friend to *Tzu Hang*, and when we looked across we saw Pwe, the Siamese cat, sharpening her claws on the cover of the mainsail. The sail-cover was put on not so much for looks as to protect the sail from the cat. As we watched we saw a man climb down on to the deck of the yacht, carrying one of the plastic bottles which we used for topping up the water tanks, and Beryl appeared in the hatch and took the bottle from him.

'I wonder who that is?' I said. 'It's not John.'

'Oh, it's just someone she's roped in,' said Clio irreverently of her mother. 'She's always roping someone in to work. Come on.'

She ran on now across the wharf to where *Tzu Hang* was lying. Although she was only fifteen she was already fully grown in height, tall and slim. She leant out from the edge of the wharf, unaware of her best clothes, and caught hold of the shrouds, and then swung on to the ratlines, and dropped down on to the deck. She wouldn't be with us on this next trip. She had been with us on all our previous trips; from England to Canada, and three years later from Canada to New Zealand, and then across to Australia, and now she had to go to England to school. We were going to follow in *Tzu Hang* as quickly as possible. She was not the first member of the crew to leave the ship, because her small brown dog, who had also been with us on all our travels, had already been sent off home from Sydney. He was travelling in luxury now in a cargo ship, spending most of the time in the bunk of one of the apprentices. We hoped to be back in time to receive him when he came out of quarantine.

To replace these two members of the crew we now had John. We had first met him in San Francisco, where we found that he also was bound for New Zealand, and like us had sailed down from Victoria in British Columbia. He was sailing single-handed in his little Laurent Giles-designed yacht, *Trekka*, which he had built himself, with great skill, in Victoria. We planned our trip across the Pacific together, and for a year now we had seen much of each other. When the two yachts lay together at the various anchorages and ports we made, John used to come on board for meals, and he would put on weight in port and take it off again as quickly during his single-handed passages. When he heard that Clio was going back to school, and that we would like to have a shot at the Horn if we could find a suitable crew to come with us, he said that he'd lay up *Trekka* in New Zealand, and come along with us. Nowhere could we have found a better companion.

Before climbing down from the wharf on to *Tzu Hang*'s deck, I had a good look at her, but I could see nothing that wanted doing now. She had been fully fitted out in Sydney, and spruced up again on her arrival in Melbourne, and she had had a good testing on her way down. She is a 46-foot ketch, 36 feet on the water line, 11 foot 6 inch beam and drawing 7 feet. She has a canoe stem and a marked sheer, and her bowsprit follows the line of the sheer so that it has a delicate upward lift, and she seems to be sniffing the breeze and eager to be off. The truck of her mainmast is 51 feet above the deck, and her mizzen 35 feet and she carries 915 square feet of sail. She is flush decked, with a small doghouse, 5½ by 5½ feet, separated by a bridge-deck from her self-draining cockpit, which is only 34 by 34 inches. She was built of teak in Hong Kong, copper fastened and with a lead keel of just over seven tons, in 1938, and she was shipped home in 1939. We bought her from her first owner in 1951, and sailed her back to Canada.

I let myself down on to the deck by way of the shrouds and went below, and I found Beryl and Clio sitting together in the main cabin opposite a stranger, an Australian and, I supposed, the man who had been helping her with the water.

'Hullo,' she said to me. 'Here you are. This is my husband. I'm afraid I didn't quite get your name——'

He introduced himself. 'How d'you do,' he said. 'I just came down here to take a snap of the *Britannia* from the wharf here——'

'And Beryl put you to work,' I interrupted.

'Too right she did, and I've been working here ever since. I tell her that there's many a firm here would snap her up, for labour management you know. She's been telling me about your trip. Sounds very interesting. I wish I could come with you.'

'As long as it's not too interesting.'

'It might be at that. It can be quite tough even round here. I do a bit of sailing here. Tasman race, but crewing, not my own boat. Which way are you going?'

'Well we thought we'd go straight across and through the Banks Strait, and then right down south of New Zealand, and then across keeping just about north of the limit of icebergs or floating ice. We'd go south of the Snares here and north of the Auckland Islands, and south of the Antipodes Islands.' I showed him the route on a weather chart.

'It's a long way south,' he said. 'Have any other yachts been that way?'

'Well one or two have been round the Horn, or through the Straits of Magellan, but I think they've all been up to Auckland first, so that our route will be a good bit further south than the others.'

'Well I'd still like to come along, but anyway I'll not say goodbye now, because I'm going to pick you all up in my car on Wednesday and drive you to the airport. I hear you are off to school in England,' he said, turning to Clio, 'I wonder how you'll like that after all this sailing.'

The tea was made and the kettle was hissing pleasantly on the galley stove, but he wouldn't stay. 'The first time I've ever known an Australian refuse a cup of tea,' I remarked, but he said that he'd have tea with us on Wednesday, and off he went.

'What a nice chap!' I said to Beryl. 'How did you pick him up? Good show fixing a lift to the airport.'

'Oh, he just came along and asked if he could give me a hand. He's brought gallons of water. And when I told him that Clio was leaving on Wednesday, he said that he'd been longing to give someone a lift as an Olympic gesture, and that we were the first non-Australian visitors that he'd been able to pick up. I don't think that he's taken a photo of the *Britannia* yet.'

We sat down to tea. 'You really ought to have been at the Games,' Clio said, 'it was such fun.'

'I don't think that I'd 've enjoyed them very much. Besides they look so like the school sports to me, and you know I hate school sports. I think the umpires are the best part. They look so funny all dressed up in their little blazers, and they go trooping after each other in single file, looking exactly like a string of cormorants, and when they sit on those steps one on top of each other, they look even more like cormorants, sitting on a rock. Anyway Pwe and I have enjoyed ourselves, and I've made a new rack for the saucepan lid.'

Beryl's carpentry suffers from her preference for using up an old piece of wood rather than throwing it away, but all the same she is a very enthusiastic and determined carpenter, and was always making something about the ship. The cat was sitting on her lap, her eyes closed and her ears pricked, and her tail lashing gently at the mention of her name. Her eyes opened now, a deep clear blue, as the ship stirred and someone stepped down on to the deck.

'Here's someone who always knows when tea's ready,' said Clio as John came down below. He was tall and fair, and filled most of the cabin door, so that Beryl had to squeeze past him to get to the kettle.

'What do you think of my saucepan rack?' she asked, pointing it out to him.

John is a carpenter, or rather an artist in carpentry. He looked at it, and then patted her on the shoulder. She looked quite small beside him. 'Pretty good,' he said, and I saw that she was pleased with the praise from the expert.

The remaining days before Clio left went all too quickly, and almost before we knew it we were standing disconsolate on the airport, watching an aircraft climbing away from the end of the runway.

'She was better than me, when I left my Mum in South Africa,' John said, 'I couldn't see for tears and fell down the gangway.' And after a moment's thought he said, 'Still she didn't really know what she was doing, did she? She kissed me too.'

'I think she had a pretty good idea,' Beryl said, and we all laughed.

Later, when we were back in *Tzu Hang*, I said to Beryl, 'Do you think she'll be worried?'

'Worried about what?'

'Oh, about us and *Tzu Hang*, you know, when she's not there.'

'No, I don't think so. As a matter of fact I asked her and she said she wouldn't be.'

'Good heavens. Why on earth not?'

'Don't be so silly. You don't want her to worry, do you? She said that she reckoned that *Tzu Hang* would look after us.'

'I hope she does.'

'Who? Clio or *Tzu Hang*?'

'Clio—or rather, both.'

In the wharf shed on the south wharf there was a small room with a telephone, which we were allowed to use. This was Beryl's operations office, and she sat there in blue jeans and a checked shirt, ordering immense quantities of stores to be delivered to the ship. When they arrived, she and John filmed each other staggering along the wharf carrying big cartons of food. John was hoping to make a complete record of the trip with his ciné camera. In the afternoons she went up to a friend's house, where she treated the eggs that we were taking with us by plunging them into boiling water for five seconds, and then into cold. It was the first time that we had tried this method of preserving eggs, and by the time we had eaten the last one it was over two months old. It still tasted good to me.

Soon after the Games were over *Britannia* left, and, as Melbourne began to reassume her workaday clothes for the few days left before Christmas, the smoke from workshops, tugs, and launches came drifting up the river, smudging the white sail-covers and making black marks on the deck. For the last few days we moved into the entrance to a little yard at the end of the wharf, as our berth was required for the dredgers, which were coming up from Port Phillip Heads. We were separated from the rest of the wharf by some high iron palings, so that casual onlookers no longer came to stand above us, and this seclusion was most appreciated by Pwe, who now spent some of the day, as well as of the night, ashore. Some shrubs grew along the palings, and there she assiduously hunted sparrows, but the Melbourne sparrows were too smart for her. Fortunately no quarantine officials found her—though there are few ships' cats who don't take a turn ashore when they get the opportunity, and no one is very fussy about them, as long as they are not mentioned.

We had one or two visitors in our new berth, and one of them was a tall elderly man, in a town suit, and a black hat, but one glance was enough to see that he was no city man. He was a sailor, and he knew a great deal not only of sail but also of the Southern Ocean. 'Well,' he said when he left, 'Good luck to you. I think you're going to need all of it, and I must say that I'd like to see another 7 feet off those masts.'

We thought that all small ship passages, at any rate long passages, had an element of luck about them—so is there about most things that are worth doing. But if we had thought that it was just a question of luck whether we would arrive or not, we wouldn't have attempted the passage. We were most certainly not in search of sensation, and we believed that we had a ship and a crew that were capable of making the passage under normal conditions. We knew of course that we might meet with bad luck in all kinds of ways, but as long as we were prepared, as far as was possible, for anything that might turn up, there seemed to be no reason why we should not overcome it.

'What on earth do you want a year's supply of stores on board for?' someone asked Beryl.

'Well,' she said, 'there is always the possibility that we might get dismasted, and then heaven knows where we might end up, and anyway the passage would take much longer than we had expected. We could probably make do for water, but I like to be sure that we have all the food we need.'

Australia was a good place to buy all kinds of tinned food, and besides tinned food we had potatoes, onions, and two sides of bacon, as well as plenty of oranges; and after the oranges were finished, we had tinned orange-juice or grapefruit-juice in almost unlimited quantity.

Although there is plenty of stowage space on *Tzu Hang*, we were so well stocked that Beryl began to think of creating more by getting rid of Blue Bear. Blue Bear had become a ship's mascot, and John and I wouldn't hear of it. He had been given to Clio when we first left England. He was a blue teddy bear, inappropriate and too big, but no artifice of ours could persuade Clio to part with him. When we were crossing the Bay of Biscay, and beating down against a south-westerly wind, with *Tzu Hang* close-hauled and sailing herself, Blue Bear, in oilskin and sou'wester, was lashed to the wheel. Through the doghouse windows we had seen a steamer come away from her course and steam up alongside to investigate. The captain came out of his cabin without his jacket, dressed in trousers and braces, to peer through his glasses, and others of the crew lined the rail. Blue Bear was obviously the centre of all interest, and when they drew away they seemed still to be discussing the composition of the crew.

He had sailed with us on every trip, lolling in one of the bunks, often with the cat and dog keeping him company, and now I found a more austere berth for him on the shelf in the forepeak, where he could still keep his eye on what went on.

There was one major difficulty to overcome before we left, and that was to get John to have his impacted wisdom tooth pulled out.

'Not likely,' said John. 'He said he'd have to dig it out, and anyway it's not hurting.'

'But you must have it done, it might blow up on the trip.'

'Not me. I don't want to have a tooth dug.'

'But John,' Beryl said, 'you sail all the way from Canada in that tiny boat, and now you won't have a tooth out. I do believe you're frightened.'

'Too true,' he said, with his usual disarming frankness, but in the end he agreed. After all there was a very pretty girl there to hold his hand. When we came back from a visit to Tasmania it was out, and John had a swollen jaw and a smug look.

Next morning I went to the Customs Office to arrange for clearance. I got into the lift and pressed the button for the appropriate floor. The lift started up and then came to a shuddering halt half way up. I tried to peer through the grille, but I was right between two floors. I thought that if I waited for long enough someone was sure to want the lift and I should be discovered without the indignity of bawling for help. After about ten minutes I heard an angry voice from below shouting, 'You up there: what are you doing in the lift?'

'I'm stuck!' I shouted indignantly.

'Well, stand in the middle, then.'

I stood in the middle, and the lift began to climb creakily upwards again. A few minutes later I was shaking hands with the Customs Officer, with my clearance in my pocket for the following day.

'I'll let the Customs launch know,' he said, 'and they'll meet you at the mouth of the river and give you a check up as you go. I remember the last chap we cleared for Montevideo was that Irishman, Conor O'Brien, some thirty years ago. He had a ship with a funny name.'

'*Saoirse.*'

'Yes, that's right. He had a beard and a yachting cap. He was a rum chap, but he was a real sailor,' and he looked at me doubtfully.

I hoped that I might be half as good, but I knew that he couldn't have had so good a crew.

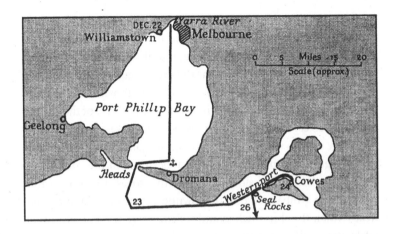

CHAPTER TWO

FALSE START

A TUG whistled down the river. Beryl sat up in her bunk as if this was the signal that she had been waiting for. She pulled a jersey over her pyjamas and went aft to the galley. I lay in my bunk. I thought that it would be the last time for days and days that I would lie in my bunk with the ship still.

John was also in his bunk, a quarter-berth that he had made in New Zealand, aft of the galley and doghouse. He had separated it from the rest of the cramped stowage space below the bridge-deck by a plywood partition running fore-and-aft from the cockpit to the bulkhead on the starboard side. Whenever I tried to get into this berth through an oval hole cut in the partition, in order to get to the stowage space aft of the cockpit, I stuck, either with my head

17

in and my stern out, or my stern in and my head out. John used to go in stern first like a wart-hog going into its burrow. Although he was bigger than I, but not taller, he did everything with an effortless grace, and could even get in and out of his berth with no apparent difficulty. It was snug inside and removed from the rest of the ship. It was his quarter—a small piece of privacy which was never invaded.

I knew exactly what was going on in the galley, without looking aft through the ship to where Beryl was sitting in the cook's seat behind the dresser and sink and beside the stoves: an oil stove and a primus on gimbals, so that they swung either way and remained steady when the ship pitched and rolled. There was an occasional rattle and clink, well-known noises which I could interpret from days of practice at sea, and then came the sudden welcome hiss of the primus burner and the sound of the primus pump. Soon the porridge was on the stove and Beryl came back to the forecabin to finish her dressing. I put on some clothes and went on deck by way of the forehatch.

It was a sparkling summer day, with a light wind blowing up the Yarra River. A little further down, a big cargo ship was docking. The tug, whose whistle had stirred us to movement, was pushing the steamer's stern in to the wharf. 'Today is the day,' I thought, 'today is the day.' And then I remembered that Pwe had not yet returned from her night out. I called her, and she answered from the shrubs by the railing. She came trotting out, explaining as only a Siamese can, about being caught out by the daylight, and about the sparrows being so wary. When she got near to the edge of the wharf, she lay down and rolled, waiting for me to come and get her. I stepped on shore and picked her up, and Beryl called 'Breakfast' from the hatch.

That wonderful call to breakfast! I do not know whether it is because of its association with porridge and bacon and eggs, but

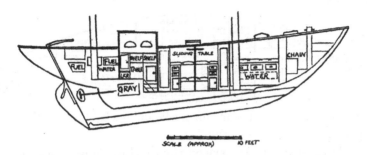

SCALE (APPROX)   10 FEET

her voice always sounds as young and exciting as ever it did, and the day seemed young and exciting too. It was an exciting day. It was the twenty-second of December, and we were starting off to England.

Our first job after breakfast was to move round to a water point on the main wharf, where we could top up our tanks. If a hose was not available we used 2-gallon plastic bottles. When we bought *Tzu Hang*, she had only one tank of 20 gallons, so that we had to fit in other tanks where we could. We put one under each bunk in the forecabin, one in the bathroom, one under the existing tank in the galley, and one in the after compartment, opposite John's berth. It was the best we could do, and it is not a bad principle to have water well divided. It is easier to check consumption, and all is not lost if a tap is knocked on and not noticed.

We carried about 150 gallons of water in these six tanks. We found that half a gallon a day per person, at sea, was a fair allowance. When we washed, we washed in salt water, and whenever possible we used salt water for cooking. Water was never rationed, but we did not waste it, and now we reckoned that we had at least a three-months' supply, and a little extra for washing if necessary.

Before we had set out on our first trip I had had a letter from Kevin O'Riordan, who had sailed across the Atlantic with Humphrey Barton in *Virtue XXXV*. He wrote, 'You will be perfectly all right provided that you have a buoyant boat, plenty of water,

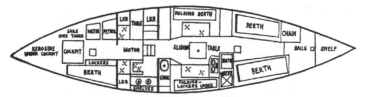

and don't mind being alone for weeks and weeks.' It seemed that all three conditions were fulfilled.

The last days before leaving on a long trip are always a rush. The whole crew spin like dancing dervishes, the list of things undone seems to grow longer instead of shorter, and everything whirls faster and faster to the climax, the moment between preparation and departure, between planning and putting into effect, the climax when a starter button is pressed, and the engine starts … or doesn't.

I always hate this moment as I'm a bad engineer, and I feel that some imp of fortune is going to decide whether we shall be permitted to cast off, or whether we shall become the harrowed and querulous prey of a thousand mechanical doubts and remain tied to the wharf that we want to leave. 'Please, engine, please start,' I beg of it in private, but on this occasion everything went well.

Beryl jumped into the cockpit and took the wheel. She put the engine astern, and we began to back out from the dock into the Yarra River. As the stream caught our deep keel it swung the stern round until we were facing upstream, Beryl then put the engine ahead and we moved slowly across to the water point on the wharf. John had walked across to catch our lines. Ever since he had joined us in New Zealand, he had taken every opportunity to work on *Tzu Hang*, making some improvement or other. Now, as she came out into the stream, he was able to look at her from a distance for perhaps the last time for many a long day. She looked fit for the sea in every way. The boom gallows could be improved; perhaps he would be able to fix it before he left the ship.

As soon as we had made fast, we began topping up the tank in use with the plastic bottles. Last of all, we filled the four bottles and stowed them below. Pwe was eager for a last run ashore, but the distance from the deck to the top of the wharf was too much for her. A tall young girl, about ten years old, with a mop of dark hair, was standing on the wharf with her father, looking down at the yacht. When she saw the cat, her eyes, which were as blue as the cat's, went round with wonder. She looked as if, more than anything else in the world, she wanted to stroke it. I climbed on to the wharf with Pwe, and held her out to her. She was too shy to speak. She stroked the cat's dark head, and longed after her when I handed her down again to Beryl.

It was time to be moving now. Beryl was at the wheel, John was ready to cast off the bowline, and the young girl's father was hoping to be asked to cast off the stern-line.

'All right, let go,' I called to John, and 'Would you mind casting off?' to the eager father.

John jumped on board and, helped by the stream, *Tzu Hang* swung out into the river and pointed her head for the sea.

Half way down to the river mouth we were met by the Customs launch. 'Thought that we'd come up and give you a tow,' they shouted as they came alongside. One of the Customs Officers came on board, and they passed us a towline.

'What can you do?'

'Eight knots,' we answered, knowing something of Australian enthusiasm. In no time *Tzu Hang*'s bow was climbing out of the water and she was foaming along, doing at least twelve knots behind the powerful launch. Every now and then she would take a sheer and, before Beryl could correct it, the towrope would tighten across the bobstay, setting the bowsprit shrouds twanging. We were soon out of the river and opposite Williamstown. We had our clearance, and the launch came alongside again to take off the Customs Officer.

'Goodbye,' they shouted. 'Good luck, come again.'

The launch curved away as they waved, ensign fluttering and brass-work shining. They seemed so typical of the Australians that we had met, friendly, efficient, and enthusiastic.

We set all sail and, close-hauled, went slowly down across the bay in the sunshine. The land and houses disappeared, the hills at the southern end of the bay were lost in haze. Here and there a few trees appeared, like a mirage on the horizon. For the rest of the day we sailed slowly across the big land-locked bay, until evening brought the lights winking out on the shore, and the channel buoys began to flash the way to the Heads. We dropped anchor off Dromana, waiting as so many sailing ships had done before, for the ebb tide to take us down early next morning to the Heads, so that we could pass through them at slack water.

Port Phillip Heads are a narrow gap, only a few hundred yards across, through which all the vast area of Port Phillip Bay pours out its waters during the ebb tide, and through which the sea comes boiling and bubbling on the flood. If the wind is against the ebb, the passage can be very dangerous. It was slack water at the Heads at ten-thirty so that we didn't have to get up early. That night *Tzu Hang* swung quietly to her anchor, as motionless as if she was still at the wharf in the Yarra River. The tide chattered busily along her planking during the night, first out to sea, and then into the bay, and then out to sea again. And in the last hour of this tide we hauled in our anchor, started the engine, and motored down the misty channel.

The buoys came up out of the murk one after the other, and we checked their numbers against the chart. The mist cleared and we could see the Heads, and as soon as we were on the right bearing we turned to run out. As we passed the signal station at Point Lonsdale we saw the signal for the tides change from the last quarter to the first quarter; it was exactly slack water and there was no ripple on the surface. On the port hand there was the black and red rusting hull of a steamer wrecked on the shoals, and ahead the sails of two yachts. As soon as we were through we stopped the engine and got up sail ourselves, but the wind was very light from the south and we made very slow progress on the port tack.

By the evening we were becalmed and the mainsail was flapping about as we rolled. We handed all sail. About midnight there was a slight breeze again and I hoisted the main. As I did so, the boom dropped out of the gooseneck, and I found that the bronze fitting on the boom had fractured. The gooseneck was frozen with rust and the bronze fitting had been bending, but, as we were close-hauled, we had not noticed it. Now it had broken and, as we were still within easy reach of a port, it was just as well to have it repaired. We should have checked and oiled the goosenecks before leaving. We turned in for the rest of the night, and early next morning set off for Westernport, a few miles down the coast and up a long arm of the sea.

The wind strengthened and we ran up the long channel against the tide, followed by the two yachts that we had seen leave the Heads before us. We tied up to a wharf at a small harbour called Cowes, leaving an anchor out to hold us off the wharf if the wind shifted. This caused great distress to the captain of a steam ferry which brought holiday-makers over to Cowes. Although he hadn't asked me to move it, he came up to me complaining angrily, as if I had already refused. I was only too anxious to move it when I found that there was a chance of the ferry fouling the line. We walked up through the village, a steep little hill, and there was a cold fresh wind blowing, which made the cotton frocks and the shirtsleeves of the Christmas visitors look out of season. At the top we found a garage and were able to get the boom fitting repaired, but it was late when we got back to the ship and, as the wind was blowing strongly down the narrow channel, we decided to leave on the tide next morning.

We had just started dinner, when there was a loud crash against the bow, and something started to scrape down the side of the ship.

'Heavens, what on earth's that?' said Beryl.

'Sounds as if we've got a visitor.'

We all scrambled up on deck as quickly as possible, including Pwe, who hates being left absolutely alone below. One of the yachts which had been tied up ahead of us had broken its stern-line and had swung round, putting its bowsprit through the pilings of the wharf, and breaking it off. We fended her off *Tzu Hang*, and while I jumped on board to look for another line, John climbed up on the wharf to get her bowline. He towed her back to her position, and we made her fast again with the best of a bad lot of line that I found in the cockpit. The wind was really blowing up and it looked as if we might have to move away from the wharf.

We settled down to dinner again, but it was a dreary Christmas Eve without Clio. Last Christmas there had been an inappropriate tree in the boat and decorations and presents and all the litter of Christmas. And now, not only were we missing the person who had made it all necessary, but we ought to have been at sea and not stuck in Westernport. John had an innate understanding of people's feelings and the good sense not to intrude upon them. He was neither unnaturally hearty nor over-sympathetic. In fact he was just himself. When Beryl offered him some brandy butter to go with his plum pudding, he said rather gloomily, 'Brandy butter, made with margarine and rum.' We all began to feel better.

Before the plum pudding was finished, there was another bump against the bow, and we found that the same yacht had joined us again. The owners arrived while we were disentangling her. They hoisted the mainsail and sailed her round into the sheltered water behind the angle of the pier, where they anchored. An hour later *Tzu Hang* began to bump against the pilings. It was raining and as black as a night can be. The lights shone on a wet deserted wharf, and the sounds of a dance band came across from the hotel.

We untangled ourselves from the network of lines and hawsers, and pushed off into the night, groping for a nine-fathom patch, with Beryl trying to take the bearings of the wharf lights on the compass and John swinging the lead-line. We could not go where the other yacht had gone as there was insufficient water, and in the end we dropped the anchor in twelve fathoms, with forty fathoms of chain, and hoped that we'd be able to get it up again in the morning.

All Christmas Day the wind blew strongly down the channel, and we stayed at anchor, very busy making everything still more secure for the journey ahead, and it was not until Boxing Day morning that we set about getting the anchor in again, in time to sail with the tide. For some time we couldn't break it out, but at last it came away, covered with thick blue clay. We unshackled it and let the chain go into the chain locker, after marking the end, and we lashed the anchor down, and fixed a ventilator over the chain navel. We expected to be well battened down for much of the way, and hoped that the ventilator would give us sufficient fresh air in the forecabin.

Meanwhile we were motoring up the channel, and in spite of a very rough short sea, with the wind against the tide, we were making good progress. By midday we were passing the lighthouse at the entrance to the loch, and we could see little coloured specks of holiday visitors all along the cliff-top. We kept under power until we were far enough out to clear Seal Rocks on the port tack, on our course for the south.

'I wonder how many rocks there are in the world called "Seal Rocks"?' said John.

'Let's hope the next "Seal Rocks" will be called "Los Lobos",' said Beryl, 'that's what they call them in South America.'

We went up and down, up and down, crunch and splash, crunch and splash, but gradually we drew clear, and then we switched off the engine. We would test it from time to time, but we would use it next, or so we hoped, to enter Port Stanley in the Falkland Islands, 6,700 sea-miles away. Up went the staysail, and *Tzu Hang* began to sail. Next the main and then the storm-jib, and we lay over and hissed away to the south. We cleared Seal Rocks easily, and *Tzu Hang* felt like a horse held in at the beginning of a long race; she seemed to snatch at her bridle, the foam flecks flying; I felt her great reserve of strength and power; she flung the wave tops behind her like fences. 'Let us go, let us go,' she seemed to say. Who could doubt that she would bring us safely home?

Beryl was at the wheel. She was wearing a yellow oilskin jumper with a hood attached and yellow oilskin trousers, and they were wet and shining with spray and from a brief shower that had passed over us; a wisp of wet hair escaped from under the hood and clung to her cheek, which was flushed with the wind, and she was radiant with delight at being off on the long trip at last. From now on she would not worry or think very much about her daughter. For the time being all her energies and thoughts would be directed to the ship and the two of us. Now that we were off she could neither write to nor hear from England, nor could she bring any further influence to bear on Clio's future, but she knew that she, more than anyone, could make this trip a success and she was going to do it.

John and I were both wearing green plastic oilskins and trousers of a strong material which we had found in New Zealand. They were called tractor suits and had stainless steel press buttons which never failed us. They had a short cape just to give a double thickness over the shoulders, but when on watch at night and in the higher latitudes, we usually wore the coats over our yellow oilskin jumpers, so that we had the advantage of the oilskin hood. John almost invariably wore a British Columbian Indian sweater, knitted from raw wool, and a knitted hat of the same material, with a round bobble on top; and I wore a red knitted sock. Both of them could be pulled down over the ears, and were often worn like this, in spite of the moronic look that they gave us. For many days to come we were not going to think very seriously about looks.

After setting the mainsail and storm-jib, John and I came aft to where Beryl had already set the mizzen, and we swigged it up a few inches. Then John took the wheel, for it was his watch. Beryl went down below, to lie in her bunk and get some rest before tea. I went below also to check the course on the chart and make the entries in the log, and from the cockpit came a great burst of song: 'Stand up and fight boy, when you hear the bell,' the words came wind-torn into the cabin. We were going to hear a lot about that bell when the going was good.

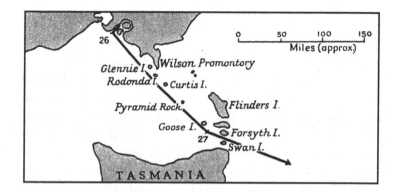

0   50   100   150
Miles (approx.)

Glennie I. Wilson Promontory
Rodonda I. Curtis I.
Pyramid Rock.
Flinders I.
Goose I. Forsyth I.
27 Swan I.

TASMANIA

CHAPTER THREE

THROUGH THE BASS STRAIT

ON my way below, I sat for a moment on the bridge-deck, the short deck which holds the mizzenmast, between the doghouse entrance and the cockpit. I put my hands on the after end of the sliding hatch, and then slipped down, taking my weight on my hands. All the same, I arrived with a bang below. This was the normal way of going down when we were in good spirits or in a hurry. At other times we would turn sideways and use the vertical steps on either side of the door in the bulkhead which led into John's compartment.

The small area which I had arrived in with a thump was the centre of the ship's activities below decks. It was 5½ by 5½ feet square, excluding portions of it which extended to the sides of the ship, underneath the deck on each side of the doghouse. It was covered by the doghouse, a low roof raised 1½ feet above the deck, in which was the sliding hatch, by which I had just come below. As we were running fast now, with the wind on the beam, I closed the hatch by sliding it back over my head, so that no spray would come in. In order to close it completely, I would have to close two small doors, but this portion of the hatch was normally left open, unless there was a strong following wind blowing coldly into the cabin.

I looked back through the small open doorway at the singer of *Carmen Jones* still in full voice, and shouted to him to stream the log. He turned to let the patent log, which was coiled ready in the stern, over the side into the water.

The doghouse was lit by two windows in each side and by two heavy ports let into its front. The ports were partially obscured by the transom of the dinghy, which was lashed down on the deck, upside down, in front of them.

While I was taking off my wet oilskin jacket, I was standing on the small space immediately above the engine. The deck here lifted up, so that I could get at the engine, or at least get at the top of the engine, when I wanted to work on it. As it had just been running, the teak deck above it was still quite warm, and the cat was making the most of it at my feet. In Canada, where we used the yacht frequently for getting to and from the island on which we lived, the cat was quite accustomed to the sound of the motor, and would sit on the engine cover, this removable piece of deck, while we were moving under power. Now that we used the engine so rarely, she would never stay below while it was running, and protested loudly to everyone about its use, and the discomforts of a deck passage. Directly it stopped, she always went below and sat on the warm cover.

Immediately in front of me and between the two ports in front of the doghouse, were the ship's clock and the barometer. They could both be seen from the cockpit, and the man on watch could see the minutes dragging slowly towards the time of his relief. The barometer was dropping slightly and I set it. Behind me was the opening which led into the after compartment, John's place, which he shared with various water tanks, fuel tanks, a large number of eggs, a 4-gallon tin of sand for the cat, four 2-gallon plastic bottles, and his own tool-box and numerous other articles, all lashed down and well secured. The well of the cockpit formed the back of this compartment, and John's berth was partitioned off on the starboard side. In order to get some light into this part of the ship, there were two dead-lights in the deck and in the front of the cockpit well there was a window. From down below, if I looked aft, I could see the helmsman's legs through this window, and when the hatch was closed and the washboards in place, it was sometimes reassuring after a heavy sea, to look aft and see a pair of legs there, solid and unmoved.

At my feet, and in front of me, there were two steps leading to the level of the main cabin, and below the clock and the barometer there was a short handrail, which we used when stepping down into the cabin. On each side, below the doghouse windows, there was another handrail, for use when moving in the doghouse. Because of the constant and often violent motion, we found these handrails most useful, and as necessary as the straps in the London Underground.

On each side of where I was standing there were two bins, the tops of which formed the bottom steps, when coming below by the more sedate method, or when going on deck. They also made two seats, where we sat for meals at sea, conveniently close to the cook and the galley. If it was very calm, or in port, we used the cabin table for meals, but if we were keeping watch and steering, it was better to use these seats, as we could shout to the helmsman, and pass him his food at the same time as those off watch were having theirs. In rough weather the helmsman would usually prefer to wait until he could be relieved for his meal.

When I stood on these two steps, with my legs straddled, and my head out of the sliding hatch, I could just see comfortably over the doghouse, with the minimum exposure. The position reminded me of the days when I used to peer out of the turret of a Sherman tank, also hoping to avoid exposure. When ducking over a steep sea there was also a certain similarity in the motion.

In front of these two seats, on the port side, was the chart table, and on the starboard side, the galley. The chart table was a large one, and under it were shelves and racks for charts, and at one end of it, against the side of the ship, there was a bookshelf for the navigational books in use. Dividers and rulers were kept in canvas bands against the bulkhead, above the table, and the sextants were in a locker just below the hatch.

The galley, on my right as I looked down into the cabin, was lined with stainless steel below and behind the two stoves. Beside them there was the cook's seat, also known as the electric chair, because the two engine batteries were below it. It faced forwards and had a curved seat, with two arms, so that the cook was held firmly in place, whatever the antics of the ship. In front of this seat was the dresser and sink, and 2 feet above the dresser, and up to the deckhead, were two shelves full of good things, such as tea, cocoa, chocolate, and sugar, and other loot for the night watches. Above the stoves were racks for saucepans and plates, and numerous mugs and cups, of a motley shape and design, hung from cup-hooks beneath them.

I hung up my coat in the oilskin locker, in front of the chart table, and then turned to the chart and laid a course down past Wilson Promontory, past Rodonda Island and the Curtis group, and up to the entrance of the Banks Strait, the southern passage through the islands, which lie between Australia and the north coast of Tasmania.

All that afternoon we made great progress, as if *Tzu Hang* was as pleased as we were to be on her way at last. The low coast to port went flying past, and in a few hours we had covered the same distance that it took two days to put behind us on our way up to Melbourne. We were under storm-jib, staysail, full main, and mizzen, and waltzing along with the sun abeam, a cold wind, sunshine, and squalls. I took over from John for the second after-noon watch from three to six. When I came up to relieve him, after making the entries in the log, he went forward to try and sweat the jib and main up a bit further. He could never leave the deck without trying to improve the set of the sails, and always the first thing that he did after coming on deck was to try and get their luffs a little tauter.

John had already fastened the wheel in approximately the right position, so that I was able to go forward and give him a hand. After working the heads of the sails up an inch or so, we coiled the ends of the halliards and hooked them up on the belaying pins on the mast. Then he went below to take off his oilskins, and I returned to the cockpit.

With the sea abeam *Tzu Hang* was going very comfortably, but every now and then a splash of spray came over the side of the ship, so that the decks were wet. None of us was ever content with the adjustment that the previous watch had put on the wheel, so I now turned my attention to try and improve the setting that John had spent most of his watch in achieving. With the wind on the beam *Tzu Hang* will not sail herself except under certain combinations of sail, and this was not one of them. On each side of the wheel, attached to the gunwale, is a piece of elastic shock cord, in turn fastened to a short piece of line with a loop in the end. These loops can be dropped over the spokes of the wheel, so that it is held in the right position but still allowed a certain amount of play. The wheel had been fixed in the position to counteract *Tzu Hang*'s tendency, under this rig, to turn up into the wind. When she is under a balanced rig, she can be left alone for hours and hours, and sometimes for days, but when artificial means are used to keep her on her course, she usually requires watching, and occasional corrections.

John appeared again in the hatchway, his arms resting on the step of the hatch. He was the carpenter, and was in charge of all maintenance, repair, and improvements, to the hull and fittings. Beryl was the mate and sailmaker, and was responsible for fitting out and provisioning the ship, and the repair of the sails. I was the skipper and navigator, and also the rigger; so that our duties were well divided. We were all adequate navigators, and often John would work out a longitude from my sight, or I would work out a position line from Beryl's.

In addition to her other duties, Beryl was also the cook, and John and I tried to recompense her in some way for her labours by being the washers-up. We sometimes offered in a half-hearted way to do something about the cooking, but she really did not trust us with the stoves, and often when something went wrong with them, we were suspect, either for having pricked them too much or not enough, during the night watch. We also took one extra three-hour watch each, so that Beryl could be free for meals and get a good sleep in the afternoon. John and I took three three-hour watches, and Beryl two, making twenty-four hours in all. Our watches always came at the same time, so that we were able to get accustomed to the hours. Beryl had the twelve to three watch at night, and always said that she preferred it, although most sailors think that it is the worst one. Even when watch-keeping was not necessary, whoever would normally have been on duty was responsible for the running of the ship. We knew automatically who had to turn out to stop a rattle or correct a course.

Now as John looked aft from the shelter of the doghouse, his eyes wandered over what he could see of the ship, he was always in search of something that he might do to improve her. Although she wasn't his, he made himself part of her, and she always came first with him. Generations of his family had followed the sea, the hard sea of Cornish fishermen and Grimsby trawlermen. Salt water was in his veins, and I sometimes wondered whether he wasn't sired in it.

He looked behind him at the clock. 'What does the log say?' he asked.

'Fourteen miles.'

'Good lass; seven knots. I streamed it two hours ago. Keep it up.'

'Are you going to turn in?'

'No, it's nearly tea-time. Those pills are good. I don't feel a thing.'

'Nor do I, but I'm going to have another tonight for luck.'

'Directly I get a chance, if it isn't too rough, I might take these doors away and put in washboards. They let too much wind in. What do you think?'

'Too much water too, sometimes. Is Beryl asleep?'

'No, here she comes. My, my!'

Beryl appeared in the hatch opening. She is inclined to let herself go over useful sea-going dresses, and I saw that she had already decided that it was cold enough for the 'Southern Ocean Cruising Rig', a combination woollen suit made up in the McLeod tartan, with a built-in belt, and a sliding hatch behind. It was practical, warm, and bright; bright yellow and black.

'How are we doing?' she asked now, that many times repeated question. I told her and she went down to make tea, and John went with her. I watched a squall dragging over the sea towards us and wondered whether it would hit us or pass behind. A few shearwaters were swinging low over the waves, but I could see no albatrosses. John stood up again and passed me a mug of tea and a slice of fruit cake. I thought that everything was very good, and best of all the fact that we were really off and laying the miles behind us. I imagined the string of dots, the daily positions, growing across the chart. 6,700 miles to Port Stanley: 67 perhaps, 67 little crosses, before we arrived. We might be there in time to send a cable for Clio's birthday. Sometimes the crosses would lie close together on the chart, and sometimes they would stretch out across it, reaching for the harbour on the other side, but the time, I knew, would pass quickly as we settled down to our sea-going routine, and cups of tea would follow cups of tea, at about this time, on each succeeding day.

The cat arrived suddenly on the bridge-deck. When any of us came on deck, we came up slowly and deliberately, taking careful hold of first the edge of the hatch and then the shrouds, but the cat used to arrive with a single spring from the chart table, so that she seemed to fall from nowhere, as light as a windblown leaf, on to the deck. The preliminaries seen from below were not so graceful. She would stand on the chart table swaying to the roll, and craning her neck as if she hoped to see where she might land, and trying to make up her mind to jump. The backstage view of her shaggy little backside, as it disappeared over the step of the hatch, couldn't compare with the arrival of the ballerina as seen from the stalls in the cockpit. She stayed with me for a moment or two, but it was too cold and rough for cats, and she returned below again.

John relieved me at six. He had had his supper and I had mine as soon as I got below. We tried to have all our meals by daylight, in order to save kerosene, and when we were keeping watch we were always ready to turn in when we could, so that the day consisted of watch-keeping, eating, and sleeping, with only a little reading before we fell asleep. As soon as washing-up was done, I opened my stretcher cot on the port side of the main cabin, and unrolled my sleeping bag and climbed in. The bunk on the other side was full of twice-baked bread, which we found didn't go mouldy, as long as it was kept in the open. We had sixty loaves.

If the bread did go bad, we had a stove in the main cabin for baking, and also for heating: a blue enamel coal- or wood-burning stove, with a good oven, but only under certain conditions could we persuade it to burn at sea without smoking.

I lay in my bunk now and tried to sleep. The water was rushing past the planking at my ear, a sweet trickling, talking sound. Soon I heard Beryl getting out the navigation lights. She lit them, waited for them to warm up, and then handed them up to John. Probably we would use them only on this night, as from now we would be off the traffic routes. Last she lit the stern light and John tied it up on the mizzen-boom gallows, a white hurricane light which never seemed to blow out, and which showed up better than the red and the green. We did not shield it from forward for this reason.

Pwe came into my bunk and sat right up by my face, her whiskers tickling my cheek, and purring loudly. She was really glad to be at sea again. It was a life that she knew and enjoyed. I think that she felt she was mistress of the ship and the people in it. One of us was always petting her or playing with her, and she seemed to think that we were hers to do what she wanted. Beryl thought that John and I teased her too much, but from the scars on my hand and sometimes my nose, I seemed to be the one who suffered. She got John once when he was teasing her, and he cut her dead for a week, and though she gradually won him back, she never used her claws on him again.

At about a quarter to nine I swung myself out of my berth and lowered my feet on to the seat below it. Then reached across to the brass pipe in the centre of the cabin, which holds the sliding table. When not in use, the table is slid up and fastened close under the deckhead, out of the way, and the pipe is used to grab on to when one is moving in the cabin. Holding on to the edge of my berth and the brass pipe, I stepped down and made my way aft. There was an oil-light burning in the cabin and another oil-light in the forecabin, where Beryl was sleeping. Both were turned down and dim, but they were there in case of some emergency.

When I looked out of the hatch, I could see John hunched over the wheel. Behind him the stern light flickered and flared, and outlined his broad figure, enlarged by an extra jersey under his oilskins. *Tzu Hang* seemed to be going at a tremendous pace, and the night looked very dark and wild. 'How are we doing?' I shouted up to him.

'Doing well,' he shouted back, 'fifty-six miles on the log. Pretty cold. No hurry.'

'Any lights?'

'Yes, you can see Glennie Island light just abeam, and Wilson Promontory ahead, only the loom of Wilson Promontory though.'

'What are the bearings?'

John checked the bearings by looking over the compass, and I marked our rough position on the chart. We were just beginning to cross the Bass Strait. I pulled on my oilskin jumper and my oilskin trousers, and then my coat and my red sock over my head, and climbed up on deck. I sat down beside John until my eyes grew accustomed to the darkness.

'I think that the wind is down a bit,' he said.

'Oh. I thought that it was blowing a little harder. All right. I can take her now.'

John stood up and stretched, then he stepped out of the cockpit and on to the deck, holding on to the shrouds and looking round him. After a time, he stepped carefully across to the hatch and disappeared below. For a time I could see his shadow moving against the lamplit wall of the doghouse, and then it disappeared and after a few minutes, I felt sure, he was asleep.

The night seemed very dark and although it was midsummer, I began to feel cold. I began to wonder why I could not see Rodonda Island. I peered under the boom but saw only universal blackness. There wasn't a star to be seen and there was no moon. Only low overcast sky and rain. I walked carefully up the deck, leaning inwards and holding on to the handrail on the doghouse, and then the handrail on the bottom of the dinghy until I could cross over to the shrouds. From there I stepped across to the staysail boom and ran my hand along this to the forestay. Looking behind the jib, I could see Rodonda quite clearly, a dark round rock of an island, and perhaps a mile away. All was well. An hour passed, and I sat in the cockpit and listened to the rush of *Tzu Hang* and the occasional spatter of spray, and I watched the dark outline of her sail against the sky. I wondered when we should see Curtis Island. After that there would be no more land until the morning. The black waves came swinging like walls out of the night and disappeared again, and sometimes they hissed quietly as they came, showing a thin white line in the darkness, or a phosphorescent glow. There was no malice in them.

I sat in the cockpit and thought of nothing in particular. I thought of Beryl in the forecabin and wondered if she was sleeping and thought that this watch was like all watches and that it was going slowly. Soon there was only an hour to go, and I went below to make myself some tea, but I kept looking aft to watch the occasional flash of a light so that I could check the course, and several times I had to climb up on deck to correct it.

I woke up Beryl and she was awake at once, and when I was back in the cockpit, I could see her shadow moving as I had seen John's below. She came and sat beside me and I felt a warm flood of companionship between us. 'The wind is up, isn't it?' she said.

'No, I think it's down now.'

I checked the log, leaning aft and flashing a torch on it. There were seventy-eight miles on the log in eleven hours, and the wind looked like holding. Beryl settled down with her hand on the wheel. She wouldn't move until she woke John at three, sitting patiently and alert at the wheel, and quite untroubled by any need for the various devices that John and I would employ to pass the time.

I turned in but could not sleep until we had seen Curtis Island. After a time, I came to the hatch again. Beryl was just as I had left her an hour before.

'Want anything?'

'No thank you.'

'Seen anything?'

'No. Sometimes I think that I see something to port, but I couldn't be sure. Now I can't see anything. Can't you sleep?'

'No, I just want to see Curtis Island. There's a creak. Have you heard it?'

'Yes, isn't it annoying? I heard a creak. I thought that it must be the mast.'

Tzu Hang never creaks in a sea, and this new noise, together with the possibility that we were being set further towards the west than I had allowed for, and consequently nearer to Curtis Island, had kept me awake. Once the noise had been noticed, it seemed to grow louder and more persistent, like a rat gnawing at a wall board. I began to imagine that *Tzu Hang* had been strained during the bashing we had given her, on our way up to Melbourne. I moved about, listening anxiously, as if I was a new and nervous father trying to discover in the middle of the night whether his offspring was really only sleeping.

Under the doghouse the noise sounded louder, and I noticed a new mug swinging on its cup-hook. I steadied it and the noise stopped immediately. It was only a rough bit of pottery in the handle, grating on the hook. I suppose it went on, but we never noticed it again. The noises of a ship blend into a tune so well known that it is never heard. Anything new strikes a discordant note which seems to vibrate through the ship as horribly as reveille to the soldier. We are often asked how we know, if we are all asleep below, if anything goes wrong, but any little change in the ship's rhythm, any slight sound, and least flap of a sail or the lift of a boom, and whoever is nominally on duty awakes immediately.

I heard Beryl call. 'Now I can see something,' she said.

I looked out of the hatch. The sky had cleared slightly, and dark against a dark sky, but clearly visible, was Curtis Island. Perhaps it was a good three miles away, but it looked much closer. I went below and fell asleep immediately and stayed asleep until I felt someone shaking me by the leg. It was John and it was also daylight. I felt as if I had dropped off for a few minutes only and quite indignant at having to get up so soon.

When I went aft to put on my oilskins, I looked out of the hatch. It was a grey morning and there were plenty of whitecaps still showing. *Tzu Hang* seemed to be going as well as ever. John was leaning over the after end of the cockpit, cleaning the face of the log.

'What have we done?'

'117. Pretty good. I think that the wind has dropped slightly, but she's still going well.'

As soon as I was ready, I climbed up the ladder and then made that familiar movement to the cockpit, one hand to the mast, one hand to the shroud, as I stepped aft. It is as well that these movements should become automatic, because they have to be carried out on black nights, with a wildly moving deck, and spray flying; when there is no room for mistakes. A great mountaineer once said that only fools and children jump on mountains, and he might have added Gurkhas, going down hill. The same applies to small ships.

For once John was content to go below without fiddling with the sails. If he was quick he would get an hour and a half before breakfast. His eyes looked slightly red on the rims, and I knew that he would be asleep in a moment. But no trump of doom, no clarion call to heaven, would bring him out of his box-like berth quicker than Beryl's call to breakfast.

I always disliked the nine to twelve watch in the evening. Between washing up after supper and the beginning of the watch, I was too wide awake to sleep, but half way through the watch I became involved in a desperate struggle to avoid it. The morning watch was far better. I was usually well rested after six comparatively undisturbed hours in my bunk, and the wonderful prospect of breakfast in an hour and a half made pleasant the worst of mornings. From seven onwards Beryl would be about and I would be able to talk to her as she appeared from time to time in the hatchway.

Until then there were many things to see and think about. First the weather portents, the barometer, the wind, the sky and the clouds, and the sea. Then the set of the sails and a quick look round for any loose ends of rope, or signs of chafe. Then a check on our position, and a search for land if we happened to be near it. Then a check on the birds that might be visible about the ship. I was always trying to recognise a companion of the day before, and often found one.

By the time all this was done Beryl appeared at the hatch. I showed her Pyramid Rock, a jagged tooth sticking abruptly out of the sea on the port quarter.

'Can you see Flinders?'

'No, not yet; I'm not sure, maybe there is something ... still poor visibility.'

She had plaited her hair and tied it over her head. It didn't look very elegant, but at sea we had to put up with it. She passed me the cat's earth, in the blue plastic basin, to empty over the side. As I handed it back, I heard the primus hissing.

A moment later Pwe arrived on the deck herself, put her paws on the cockpit coaming, just aft of the doghouse, and looked at the weather. She decided that it was too wet to keep to the deck and went below again. Here she did all that was possible to interfere with the cooking, protesting her hunger in a loud voice, and jumping on to Beryl's back, if she got the chance, in order to explain her need more lucidly.

I heard Beryl call that breakfast was ready and, without any delay, John appeared and handed me a bowl of porridge with milk and brown sugar. If *Tzu Hang* had been sailing herself he would have stayed in bed, and I would have handed him his food into his berth. Now he sat down on the step at the foot of the ladder and Beryl, who almost always does two things at once, sat in the cook's chair and read, and at the same time fried bacon and eggs. From time to time she gave the cat a piece of fried bacon rind from the pan, and Pwe would pat it about the deck with her paw, till it was cool enough for eating. If we were having cooked bacon, Pwe would not

42

dream of eating the rind unless it was cooked also. After bacon and eggs came burnt toast and home-made marmalade. Burnt toast is the hallmark of Beryl's wonderful breakfasts, as inseparable from them as her book is from her, when she is cooking.

These typical breakfasts were provided for us day after day for fifty days all across that great Southern Ocean. Perhaps never before had such good breakfasts been eaten so regularly for so long in those particular waters.

After breakfast we could see Flinders Island indistinctly, and soon we began to try to pick out the entrance to the Banks Strait. After a time we could make out a small mark on the horizon ahead which took form gradually. A lighthouse, a black lighthouse instead of a white one, as described in the pilot book, but a lighthouse all the same, on a low flat island. It was Goose Island, and as we rounded it we entered the Banks Strait.

Then came another marvellous day of sailing. Forsyth Island to port and the green Tasmanian Coast away to starboard, and the boom as wide as could be in order to let us get round Swan Island. There was white water showing everywhere as we squeezed past. By noon, when we reset the log, we had done 163 miles. By four o'clock in the afternoon, we had to haul down the mizzen and shortly afterwards we handed the main, running under the two headsails, whereupon the wind began to ease, as it so often does in the evening, and we set the main again.

The Sydney-Hobart race had started on the same day as we did, and we had wondered at one time whether we would have to pass through them. We heard in the evening, on the radio, that the leaders were not yet into the Bass Strait, and were meeting with light winds only. We were lucky to be on the top side of a depression which would, with any luck, carry us most of the way across the Tasman Sea.

By midnight when Beryl relieved me, the wind was right aft with an awkward sea running. It was necessary to steer all the time, and we had rigged preventer guys so that the boom would not smash over if *Tzu Hang* gybed. As she rolled in the steep following sea, the boom would try to lift against the preventer guy, and sometimes the leach of the sail would give a flap, which set the helmsman to spinning the wheel frantically. There was no need to worry with either Beryl or John at the wheel.

All through the dark and windy night, as the white wave tops marched in luminous procession past the ship, bright green bars of phosphorescence shone suddenly out of the night and fell astern, glowing like emeralds between the black breasts of the waves. They were beacons for *Tzu Hang* pointing her way to the south.

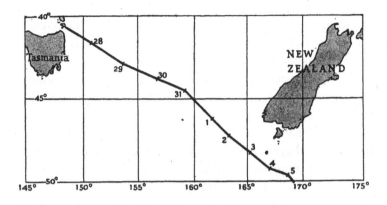

ACROSS THE SOUTH TASMAN

NEXT morning *Tzu Hang* was still racing along, with the wind a little too far aft for comfort. The glass was low, and the wind's grey horsemen, the low rain clouds, came riding up from behind throwing a lash of rain across us as they passed, while the albatrosses ranged like greyhounds in front of them, across the downland of the sea. Wherever we looked we would see somewhere the sudden tilt of an albatross's wing, as it turned to sweep down and along the moving valley of the sea.

Perhaps I was thinking of albatrosses, but at any rate I wasn't paying sufficient attention to the steering, and allowed *Tzu Hang* to slew as a wave passed, so that there was a sudden wump as the boom went over in a gybe. The preventer guy had parted and the boom came over with a bang against the backstay, but the initial shock had already been taken by the preventer guy, and no damage was done, except to my reputation with the rest of the crew. I started to haul in on the main-sheet but before I was finished, *Tzu Hang* rolled and the boom gybed back again.

Two faces appeared almost immediately at the hatch opening. Neither of them said anything, but I said, 'I think that we'll have the main down now and set the twins.' When it was all finished John said, 'Thank God it was you and not me.' The thought of the accidental gybe stayed with him all the day, and seemed to give him ill-suppressed satisfaction, and in the evening he said, 'You know, I haven't really felt right since I let *Tzu Hang* gybe on that rough night going into Auckland, and now thank goodness you've done one.'

'Not one, two, and only a few seconds between. You'll never beat that.'

'No, thank goodness. I really feel fine about it now.'

Beryl looked rather smug. I think that she was the most careful helmsman of the three of us.

Tzu Hang was rigged in those days with a topmast forestay from the top of her mast to her bowsprit, a jibstay which hauled out on a traveller on her bowsprit, and a forestay which went to a fitting on her bow. The twin staysails were set on separate twin forestays bolted through a deck-beam half way between the bow and the mainmast, and on booms from a mast fitting 5 feet above the deck. When they were not required, these twin forestays were fastened out of the way of the staysail boom to the pinrails near the shrouds.

When we were running under twin staysails, the sheets from the booms led back to a block, and then to the tiller, so that *Tzu Hang* steered herself. It usually took us about twenty minutes to change from fore-and-aft rig to running rig, from the time we went on deck to the time we went below, and we were always doing it.

We had not yet changed the wheel for the tiller, and self-steering would not work with the wheel, but now there was no further danger of a gybe, and the ship could be left to herself for short periods. It was much easier on the helmsman, but the sail area was reduced and we were not going so fast.

Not going quite so fast, but very nearly, because at noon we had 153 miles on the log, and by three in the afternoon it was blowing force 7, and *Tzu Hang* was beginning to sit up on the wave tops and to rush forward on them in the most exhilarating way. One wave top climbed on board just in front of the cockpit and we seemed to be wrapped in the breaking crest. We handed the twin staysails and ran under bare poles until after tea, when we set the twins again.

For the next few days we were caught up in a relentless rhythm of the sea. The ship reeled and surged and swung away on her course; the glass rose slightly and fell again, as depression chased depression across the Tasman Sea; rain squall after rain squall followed short sunlight, and we climbed repeatedly on to wet decks for our three-hour watches and, sleepy and chilled, down again at the end of them. The glass stayed low, and everything below decks became damp and sodden. The shifts in the wind kept us busy with sail changes. For most of the time we were under twins, but when the wind came abeam, we dropped the weather staysail and took the pole out from the other, sheeting it home as a reaching sail. Then we set the storm-jib and mizzen, and that was all that we needed. When the wind was aft, and provided it was not too strong, we set the mizzen as well as the twins.

New Year's Eve, five days out, 750 miles on the log, and a black wet night. We had Christmas pudding for dinner; the first of the six Christmas puddings that we had for celebrations, and which would mark the small achievements of our passage. John and I were always trying to get Beryl to produce them, but they were rigorously controlled. As I sat up in the rain in the night watch, I thought of the previous New Year's Eve, which the three of us, and Clio, had spent high up on a mountain ridge in Maui. I thought of her in England and wondered how she was getting on, and thought also that however keen I was to make a quick passage back to join her, I would also like to have a break in this wet rushing movement. At twelve I went forward and shook Beryl: 'Happy New Year!'

'Oh, Happy New Year!' she said, and was awake immediately. I had a wet towel round my neck, five days' grizzled grey beard, and wet oilskins, and as I leant forward to give her a kiss, she felt warm and damp and smelt slightly musty.

Back in the cockpit another black rain squall was marching up from behind, dark and forbidding, and by the time Beryl joined me it was sluicing round us.

'How are you feeling?' I asked her.

'Feeling fine; still I wouldn't mind a change so that we could fix up the tiller for self-steering.'

'Me too, everything's so damned wet.'

Wet or no, it made no difference while the wind lasted. Sleep and feed and watch; too little sleep, enough food, and too much watch, but by the end of the first week, we were still just short of a thousand miles: four miles short. We were also rather further north than we had intended as a northerly current was setting us up and knocking some miles off the run as measured on the chart. On that last day we were close-hauled under jib, staysail, and mizzen and with the wind from the south, but for the first time since we left Westernport, *Tzu Hang* was sailing herself, and what a blessed change we all thought it was. We were all down below.

'This is more like it,' said John. 'That was really too much like work.'

'Good heavens, I thought that all you single-handers were gluttons for punishment. Beryl and I never do that sort of thing. It was only because you were there that we didn't stop and take it easy for a time.'

'No,' said John, 'I suppose that it's the cold and the damp, and such a long spell of it, but I wouldn't like to go on indefinitely with weather like that. If she'll steer herself it's another story.'

'The glass is shooting up, so maybe we can fix the tiller tomorrow.'

We all slept a glorious and undisturbed sleep that night, and woke up to find that the sails were flapping uselessly. We took everything down while the porridge cooked, and after breakfast set about changing the wheel to the tiller. At first it seemed as if we would be unable to do so, as the wheel fitting was frozen hard on to the rudder-post, and we had to heat it with a blow torch before we could move it. Wheel, wheel-box and worm-gear we stowed right aft in the counter, and put the tiller on in its place. *Tzu Hang* looks rather better with a tiller, or perhaps it is just that a change is nice.

While we worked a seal played around us, popping his whiskery nose out of the oily sea, and looking like a bald-headed old man, peering over the morning paper; then he turned over on his back and waved a flipper across his chest as if he was fanning himself. After a time he went on his way. Perhaps he was bound for the Snares, but anyway he didn't seem to be at all perturbed about his landfall.

While the seal played around us the albatrosses came visiting. They came gliding over the swell, apparently using the cushion of air, raised by the lift of the waves, to support them. There seemed to be no breeze at all, and from time to time they were forced to give a few slow strokes with their wings. They always seemed to look rather furtive and ashamed when they did so, as if they hoped that no other albatross had seen them. It was obviously something that they did not want talked about in the albatross club. They glided so close to the smooth water that sometimes an end wing feather would draw a skittering line across the surface as they turned. One after another they came up to the ship and thrusting their feet out in front of them, they tobogganed to a halt and as they settled down, they held their wings together high above their bodies, until they folded them one after the other, in a curious double fold, against their backs.

They paddled round the ship as we worked, coming close under the counter, and all the time Pwe pursued them on deck. She crouched under the rail and then raised her head, with her ears flattened sideways, so that she showed as little of herself as possible when she looked over. Then she crouched down and crawled along the deck until she thought that she was directly over one of the big birds, when she looked again. But she could get no further, and her jaw used to chatter with rage and frustration.

Sometimes the albatrosses used to dip their bills in the water and then snap them together with a popping sound. They reminded me of the senior members of a Services Club, tasting port. We never found out what they ate. They trifled with pieces of bread, but never swallowed them.

As soon as we had fitted the tiller, John turned his attention to the washboards, which he made from some spare teak that we had on board. He made a perspex window in the lower washboard so that we could look through to see how the helmsman was and if he needed anything. While he was doing this, Beryl was working on some caulking, stopping a slight leak in the deck, and I was greasing rigging-screws.

When John worked with wood, he seemed to caress it. The tools in his hands looked as if they carried out his wishes of their own volition, and even the wood seemed to submit without protest. His movements were so sure that any work he was doing appeared amazingly easy. When he marked wood with a pencil, he marked it with one straight line, and when he picked it up again after laying it aside, he knew exactly what his marks meant. Most wonderful of all, everything always seemed to fit. Now he rebated the two washboards so that they overlapped and made a windproof joint, and when he dropped them into position in their slots they fitted as if the join had been a straight saw-cut.

'How on earth do you get things to fit the first time?' I asked him.

'I reckon that's what you learn in five years' apprenticeship,' he replied.

He was sharpening his chisel on a stone with regular even strokes, the angle never varying. When he finished the light shone on one smooth face, and not on a number of facets, as it would have done if I had been doing it.

'When I was doing my apprenticeship,' he went on, 'and finished my first job, I went to the foreman and asked him to pass it. It was a small cabinet and I was pretty proud of it. He came and looked at it, and then went away without saying anything, and came back in a few minutes with an axe and smashed it. Then he told me to make a proper one. I guess that makes you learn to do a thing properly. Still everyone can't be a carpenter. You have to be the right type you know.'

He said this as if he was commiserating with me for being blind or a cripple, and he was hoping for some reaction on my part.

When John had been a youngster in Jersey, the Germans had moved in and, owing to some failure of an engine in a small boat, he and his mother and father were unable to get away. The whole family were then taken to Germany and held throughout the war as hostages. John's father has been described to me as a sturdy and uncompromising Yorkshireman, and I'm sure that John is very much a chip of the old block, so that the Germans must often have regretted their selection. What with one thing and another, John did not have a great deal of opportunity for orthodox schooling, so that when he found himself back in Jersey, he decided to learn a trade. When he had finished his apprenticeship, he went to South Africa with his mother to her people, as there were only two of them then, and after a time he set off by himself to Canada, to work as a carpenter and to build his boat, and to sail her round the world if possible. We were lucky to meet him soon after the beginning of his journey.

If the first week was all that we had expected of the South Tasman, the next week, which was spent largely south of New Zealand, gave us all kinds of variety. After the day of rest and repair in the sun, we had a grey wet drizzling day, with the wind in the north-west and continuous rain. We fixed a plastic water-bottle to the foot of the mizzenmast, and fastened a sail-cover upside down under the mizzen boom. We caught two gallons of water, and on the strength of this I shaved, and decided never again to go unshaven for so long, if I could avoid it. My beard felt dirty. It probably was, and it tickled me when I tried to sleep. From then on John and I kept our whiskers more or less under control.

The next day was warm and sunny, with a light following wind. John was the photographer, and he had about 2,000 feet of 16 mm. film which he intended to shoot. Now he suggested that we should put the dinghy overboard and film *Tzu Hang* under her twins. There was little wind. *Tzu Hang* was rolling along very quietly, and there was no white water, only the long easy swell. There seemed no danger in putting the dinghy over, and if he got left behind we would put the headsails down and wait for him.

We had two dinghies on board, stowed one on top of the other, upside-down. The bottom of one was of moulded fibre-glass, light and fast and easy to handle. It has stood up to an immense amount of rough use for several years, and was easily pulled on board by one person. On top of this was a plywood pram, also light and seaworthy and with a high freeboard, so that it fitted down on the deck. Stowed upside-down it looked splendid and conformed to the lines of the doghouse. Moreover, it had two handrails running along its bilges. In the water and the right way up, it looked rather like a pale blue bath, but it was a great load-carrier and a good seaboat, and provided there was no head wind and a light load, it was easy to send through the water. John had carried an outboard engine on *Trekka*, and during the Pacific crossing, and in New Zealand, we had done some great trips with it and John's outboard.

We undid the lashings and prised the boat off the fibre-glass dinghy, to which it was clinging like a limpet. Then we unfastened the life-line and dropped it over the side. John jumped in and we handed him his movie camera in a plastic bag. He took the oars and rowed away from the ship and as the wind had dropped altogether now, we saw that he could row faster than we were sailing. He rowed on ahead of us, working hard, and was soon far enough away to leave his oars in the rowlocks and start filming. Completely alone, in a pale blue bathlike boat, and on a vast and slowly heaving sea, he looked like something out of a nursery rhyme. An albatross landed beside him and pecked at an oar. *Tzu Hang* rolled slowly past him as he filmed, and when he was about a hundred yards behind her and had taken a shot as she went behind a swell, he rowed up after us. We all had a go then. It was a fascinating sight to watch the ship rolling slowly along in this big smooth swell. The motion, which we had become accustomed to, looked tremendous from the dinghy. She was showing a vast amount of copper paint as she rolled, and it was still very clean, with only a few goose-barnacles visible here and there. Nothing seems to be able to defeat goose-barnacles. I believe that they would grow on pure arsenic. When we were sailing up to Canada, the log-line became so fouled with them that we had to change it. We left the old line in the stern so that they would dry up and we could then rub them off, and the cat used to eat a few off the line every day. Above the copper there were some signs of green weed clinging to the bottom of the white paint, but otherwise *Tzu Hang* was looking quite yachty. She had had a complete refit in Sydney. As I was thinking about all this, she drew away from me and I had a sudden panic feeling of being deserted, and rowed as hard as I could after her. Although there was no wind, she seemed to be going quite quickly through the water.

Beryl got in the dinghy and rowed away as if she had spent her life on the open ocean in one, but when she was back on board, I understood exactly the feelings of an old hen foster mother, when the last of its ducklings is back again from the water and safely under its wing. *Tzu Hang* seemed to do so too.

Next day was Sunday and we were becalmed. We were busy with all kinds of work on the deck. John painted the washboards, I finished the rigging-screws, and Beryl was still hunting for and recaulking small deck and skylight leaks. It was warm on deck and not at all the weather that we expected so far south. It didn't seem to go with this sea, which the great grain ships used to cross. I wondered how often, just in this bit of water where we were sitting in the sun, a square-rigged ship had flung past, down to her topsails, and wondering whether she was south of the Snares and north of the Auckland Islands. A number of sailing ships were wrecked on the Auckland Islands, and although there are 140 miles between them and the Snares, they are better behind than in front, when visibility is bad. We were approaching the dotted line on the chart, which is inscribed, 'Icebergs and loose ice may be met with south of this line'.

We had lunch on deck. Lunch was always cold and consisted of twice-baked bread, which was holding up well, butter, cheese, jam, salami or sardines, fruit cake, and an orange. Sometimes we had soup, and we had orange juice or grapefruit juice to drink. We also had a large supply of onions which we ate raw with our cheese.

During the morning John had taken some shots of all the activities on deck, while Pwe spent her time hunting the albatrosses with her usual ineffective procedure. I remembered the reporter in Seattle who had telephoned me for a story, and who had said, 'Say, Captain, will you tell me what you folks do all the time, just laze around and lounge about on deck?'

After lunch I upset the linseed oil over the newly painted washboards. John didn't even say, 'Some mothers have them,' as he was heard to do when I pushed a screwdriver through my finger in Honolulu. He said, 'I've got to paint them again anyway,' and Beryl thought that it would do the deck good. It was quite obvious that everyone was determined that 'crew trouble' wouldn't mar the trip. The washboards never did get painted again because this was the last of the paint-drying days.

Next day we had a wind from the north-east and we made sail after breakfast, under full sail and the Genoa. The sea was calm and there was the same long swell. *Tzu Hang* sailed along unattended all day. I did 'laze around all day', but Beryl and John must always be at something. John had persuaded Beryl to knit him a Fair Isle jersey, and they were now busy trying to work out the pattern.

Pwe was full of activity also. She kept dancing up to us sideways, her ears back and her body arched, daring us to do something.

It was about this time that she invented her main game. Siamese cats are not very original in their ideas about games, and this was inevitably a mouse game. She would fly up into my berth, a canvas bunk on two poles, and then stare over the pole at her victim. If he did not respond she would complain vocally, but none of us could resist her. The game consisted of running a finger along under the canvas, while she pounced on it. There were two variations; one was to run a finger along the side of the pole, while she hid inside and tried to grab it by putting her arm over the pole, and the other was for her to sit at the end of the berth and await for a finger to appear from under the canvas. This was extremely tense work and as the finger approached the end of the berth, excitement grew to fever pitch with both participants. She never let it get the better of her, and although she always caught it, she only dabbed the finger with a paddy paw. After she had caught it, she would swagger away, like a boxer who has floored his opponent.

In the afternoon we heard a soft sigh come faintly through the hatch, and then another, and another, and knew that we had a school of porpoises with us. We went on deck and John filmed them, crisscrossing in front of the bow and breaking water together in threes and fours. Sometimes they would haul off to one side or the other, and one of them came leaping along almost continuously out of the water, and falling over on to his side at each jump. They stayed with us for some time, but eventually tired of the play, and dropped astern, lazily rolling a dorsal fin out of the water, before they went off on some other business. Pwe stood with her forefeet on the cockpit coaming to watch them, with her ears pricked and in a rather alarmed and elongated attitude. They are horrible animals, she thinks, and will never venture further on deck if they are about. We always love their visits, they are such merry creatures, and feel strangely gratified by their attentions, and sorry when they leave.

The blue whale also seems to be a friendly animal, and is the only whale that likes to accompany us. We have seen quite a lot of them, sometimes longer than *Tzu Hang*, and they have often steamed alongside, to the delirious excitement of Clio's small brown dog.

We were now 200 miles south of the south-east corner of New Zealand, in longitude 170° east and latitude 50° 30′ south, and the wind was freshening from the north-east. On January 8, with the wind still blowing freshly from the same quarter, we were nearly down to 52° south. We could not make much headway against a roughish sea, and the starboard tack would take us back to New Zealand, while the port tack would take us further down towards the iceberg zone. I felt that there were enough hazards without going further south, where we risked the chance of meeting up with some ice, and I didn't want to lose any sea that we had gained. So we hove to and waited for the weather to change. For the last two days of the second week we lay hove to. It was the dreariest period of the whole trip: cold, and grey, and uncomfortable.

I am sure that Beryl and John would have preferred to have continued further south, and perhaps I was exaggerating the danger of running into ice, but at any rate they showed no signs of impatience. Beryl was soon enmeshed in reams of multi-coloured wool for John's jersey, and John was occupied in making some ingenious device out of copper, a belt-buckle, I believe. Of all the many things which tax one's patience on a long trip of this sort, the hardest to bear is failure to make progress in the right direction; I sought refuge in the country with Soapey Sponge and Lucy Glitters.

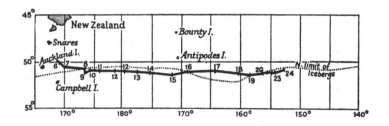

CHAPTER FIVE

INTO THE SOUTHERN OCEAN

THE third week started with another dull drizzling day, with the wind veering to the east, so that we were able to make sail at ten in the morning, and for a short time we sailed to the north. Soon it began to rain harder, and the wind to swing to the south, and by three in the afternoon we decided to set the twins again. While Beryl and John were hanking the sails to the forestays, I led the sheets through the blocks on the deck and back to the cockpit. As I was making the sheets fast temporarily to two cleats on the deck, I saw a number of white horses away in the south-west. The sky was beginning to break up and the rain had stopped, and the whitecaps began to spread across the sea and to advance towards us.

'There's a packet of wind out there,' John shouted back to me, and almost as he said it, a blast of cold air straight from the icefields struck us. The staysails were half way up and began to shake violently and the booms to leap wildly up and down. I hauled the sheets in as tightly as I could, first one and then the other, and only brought the booms under control with difficulty. Beryl and John doubled up on the halliards to get the sails set, and then came aft, laughing with the excitement of the struggle with the sails and the cold wind, to help me with the sheets.

The difficulty now was to transfer the sheets from the cleats, to which they were fastened, to the tiller. Beryl and I hauled on one sheet while John took a quick round turn and a draw hitch to the tiller. Directly Beryl and I let go, the pull came on to the tiller, and John could only hold it, in spite of his strength, with the greatest of difficulty. Beryl and I then took the tiller and forced it over against the pull of the sheet, until the ship began to turn to port against the port staysail. This split the wind out of the starboard staysail, and as it began to flutter, John hauled the sheet tight, and made it fast to the tiller in the same way. Now we had an equal pull on the tiller, and if it turned out that the tiller was not quite in the centre, the adjustment was fairly easy once the sheets had been transferred to it. This was a strong wind and made setting up the twin staysails much more difficult than usual.

We had terylene sheets and, unless they were fastened with a round turn and a draw hitch, they jammed so hard that it was almost impossible to undo them. The draw hitch never slipped. Although we had a great deal of wind from easterly quarters during the first half of the voyage, we used the twins more than any other sails during the passage. The sheets passed through two blocks and over the cockpit coaming, which was cut away and sanded down to take them. Beryl was continually putting tallow on the sheets, and as a result, in spite of the continuous movement and tension, they were undamaged by chafe.

It was good management to change to the twins just at the beginning of my watch, because now we could all go down to tea. We got the fire going in the saloon and it was warm and snug. We still had to keep watches because we were below the iceberg limit, but the ship was steering herself and the wind was in the west.

A sailor, or at least a navigator, is always conscious of the land about him. The sea may be empty and clear from horizon to horizon, yet he will know that just here or just over there, is the land. Sometimes, when no land is visible, he will feel hemmed in by it, and sometimes he will be conscious of the sea's great deserted loneliness. I had never had the feeling of loneliness in the Atlantic or the Pacific. Here was a steamship route, there an island, and over us an aircraft might pass. Although for days and days we had seen nothing, we had always been aware of man moving or living not too far away. Now, as we entered the Southern Ocean, with New Zealand behind us, there was a feeling of desertion and loneliness. The Chilean coast was over 4,000 miles away, and in all that sea probably no ships at all. The only living things above the waters were the wheeling, wandering birds. Because we had just been struggling with the wind together, and because we had achieved what we were trying to do, and the ship was flying along on her course, we felt at one with the ship and at one with each other. This feeling of companionship was strong between us. Of course we never mentioned it, but I think there was a feeling of affection between all of us, quite apart from Beryl being my wife, because we were the only human beings there, because we were a team, and because we were managing.

That day a new seabird arrived: a dark brown mottled bird, a cross between a hawk and a gull, with white crescent markings on his wings, and a fast wing-beat. He looked as if he might like to sit on ice from time to time, and somehow I didn't like him. He was a great skua. We also saw a small branch which must have drifted from Campbell Island.

Next morning we found the wind going round to the north-east and, while John had his after-breakfast sleep, Beryl and I set the mizzen and Genoa instead of the twins. We were making splendid time, with an easy sea, but the wind continued to veer until we were close-hauled and under all sail. By nine in the evening we had made sixty-five miles on the log since noon, but we were still down below the northern limit of the iceberg drift, and we could not do better than a little south of east. The ominous skua was round again, showing clearly the white crescent markings on his wings.

It was a good night. We were close-hauled, reasonably steady, and the Genoa showed taut and white in the moonlight. It was a new terylene sail. The motion was easy, and the water rushed pleasantly past the planking. I sat below the doghouse ladder while the kettle heated on the oil stove. From time to time I looked out. The moon was right on the bow, throwing its bright reflection along the sea, a path for *Tzu Hang* to sail down. Down below, if I looked forward through the main cabin, I could see the dim light in the forecabin where Beryl was sleeping. I could make out the blue cover on the unused bunk, and faintly the impassive wooden face of a Hawaian girl, carved out of a piece of driftwood, which we had got in Hawaii, and which was fastened to the bulkhead by the doorway leading into the forepeak.

In the forepeak itself there was a jumble of sails; the twin staysails, the storm-jib, the working jib, and the two little topsails which we never used. On the one side was the chain locker and on the other side were store cupboards, with tools and spare parts on a shelf over them. Right in the bow there was a large shelf of stores, not immediately required, and wedged behind the samson post, another tin of earth for the cat. Somewhere also there was sixty fathoms of 3-inch manilla rope, and presiding over all, on top of the shelf in the bow, sat Blue Bear.

I took another look round and went forward to wake Beryl for her watch. I didn't bother to look out again but turned in to my bunk. As Beryl walked aft, she put the cat on my chest. She started to purr, as if she was trying to tell me how very pleased she was to be able to pay me a visit, and she tickled my face with her whiskers, until I lifted the edge of my sleeping bag and allowed her to creep inside. She was still purring and exploring the inside of the bag when I went to sleep.

I awoke to a thump which shook the whole boat so that my first idea was that we had struck some ice. Almost at once I heard John shouting, 'On deck, on deck!' Beryl and I jostled together for the ladder, but the McLeod tartan fell behind at the corner, because she stayed for a moment to grab her boots. The mast was shaking, and there was a flapping and rustling noise, as if a sail had carried away. When we got out we found the Genoa streaming away to leeward. The pin of the sheave on the outhaul on the bowsprit had sheared, and the Genoa was now free except for the sheet and the halliard. The sheet was flapping wildly and the sail flying loose. We lowered away and hauled it in, and soon had it under control again. We lowered the mizzen and *Tzu Hang* continued to sail as before on the same course, but at much reduced speed. John kept saying, 'Something hit me on the head. It must have been the sheave. I can't think why it didn't do me more damage.' We went to look in the cockpit, but found only the head of the bolt which had sheared. The sheave must have flown like a bullet to sea. Anyway, we had a spare one, and after breakfast John cut and drilled two cheek pieces to hold it. He made them out of brass sheet.

After it was finished we set the storm-jib. 'Not the storm-jib,' said Beryl, who is really of the hang-on-and-blow-them-away school. She is also the sailmaker, so she has conflicting interests. Still the glass was dropping, and we set the storm-jib. By the afternoon we had reefed the main. In spite of the reduction in sail we had made 146 miles by midday.

In the afternoon the weather turned cold and blustery, and the wind, which was going slowly to the north, was bringing dark storm-clouds with it. The sea had an angry look, and there were many whitecaps; sudden gusts, which found their way round the shoulders or down the face of the swells, sent little wavelets on the tops of the waves scurrying hither and thither across the surface. In order to let John and Beryl finish their watch below, I decided to put off reefing again, and handing the staysail, until the change of the watch.

An hour before it was time to call them there was another sickening thump and a jerk, and I saw something fall from the main cross-trees to the deck, and the main after shroud go slack. I put *Tzu Hang* round quickly on to the other tack and hove her to. By the time John and Beryl were up I found that the shackle which secured the after main shroud to the mast fitting had broken. *Tzu Hang*'s biggest weakness was that the main shrouds were shackled on to lugs at the mast fitting, and that the size of the holes in the lugs limited the size of the shackles, so that they were in fact too weak for the rigging. We lowered the main and the staysail, leaving *Tzu Hang* hove to under the jib only. Then we fastened a line at the top of the shroud and below the eye, and took it over the cross-trees and down to a tackle on the deck, and hauled it as tight as possible. John went up with a file and for over half an hour, standing on slack ratlines, with one arm round a wildly swaying mast, he struggled to file the hole in the lug big enough to take a larger shackle. It seemed an interminable time before it was finished, and all the time the cold rain and sleet whipped our faces and numbed our hands. As soon as the pin fitted, we slacked away on the weather rigging-screws, and then hauled down on the tackle until the eye was near enough for the shackle to be screwed up. Then we set up all the rigging-screws, double-reefed the main and set *Tzu Hang* on the right tack again, leaving her to sail herself while we made tea.

'Hope we don't have another day like this,' said Beryl.

'Tomorrow's Saturday again,' I said, 'because we are just about crossing the date-line. We may have to go through it all again.'

'Anyway, we've got John.'

'Good old John. Well done, boy!'

John shook his head and clicked his tongue, 'I don't know how you old folks managed before I came,' he said.

Tzu Hang sails well in a strong blow, under double-reefed main and storm-jib, and if she cannot carry this amount of sail it is time to stop. The next few hours were some of the roughest that she has ever given us. The north-easterly wind had set up a short sea against the south-westerly swell, which never seems to disappear. *Tzu Hang* was flinging herself into the waves and bucking over them, and sometimes she seemed to take to the air altogether. The rice was thrown out of the pan in which it was cooking, and the pans were thrown off the stove. We turned in, but it was impossible to sleep. Yet gradually the thumps and crashes died down, and by midnight, as we sailed into a new day and yet the same day, the sea and wind were easier. Nine months before we had crossed the date-line in the opposite direction on our way to New Zealand, 1,400 miles to the north. We thought that it was quite cold and rough then also.

The second Saturday gave us as big a contrast as ever one gets at sea. We were soon under all sail with a northerly wind and sunshine. The low cloud and poor visibility had vanished, and now, a mile away, an albatross's wing would show suddenly like a spar against the sky, so that we would look again to see we knew not what, thinking perhaps of a small ship like ourselves, but only to see the empty sea and the swoop and soar of the birds. They kept gliding past us in a lazy inspection of all that went on in the ship, momentarily losing their balance in the air disturbed by our sails.

Pwe came out to sun herself on the deck. She took this business of sunning herself very seriously—not as if she really enjoyed it, but rather as if it had been recommended by her doctor. She would find somewhere out of the wind and sit with her eyes shut. The moment some spray came on the deck, or the wind ruffled her fur, she would give up in disgust. Her earth was put every day in a blue plastic bowl, chosen to match her eyes, and was usually kept under the chart table. If by any chance Beryl forgot to change it, she would go to her and complain bitterly. On fine days it was put on the bridge-deck and it was great fun to see her sitting on it and swaying to the roll of the ship at the same time. If ever she wanted any help or comfort, she would go to Beryl, but for sport she came to us.

Tzu Hang sailed herself all through a perfect sunny day, with a slight swell from the north and a long swell from the south-west. We had a smart little grey gull with us, white underneath with a prominent black eye, like a shearwater in shape but not so big. In the afternoon we saw ten albatrosses on the water in a discussion group over a piece of seaweed. They are the most curious of birds, but almost everything must be a novelty to them in that endless empty sea.

On Sunday we were sailing again with the Genoa, and in sunshine. John wanted to film *Tzu Hang* under this sail, so we put him overboard again in the dinghy. Just before we put the dinghy overboard, we saw three small brown whales lying together on the surface of the sea. Their colour was most striking, a light

65

reddish brown. They are known as 'white' whales, and have this habit of congregation. We sailed up to them before launching the dinghy, hoping to get a film of them, but they sounded before we got near enough. We were sailing well, so that once the dinghy was in the water we quickly left it behind. It soon disappeared behind the long swell and looked absurdly small when it reappeared. We went about and sailed back past it, and then about again, and hove to while John came on board. Although there was no danger, I had felt irrationally anxious, I suppose because of the size of the swell, and also because of this ever-present feeling of loneliness. It must have been the smallest boat ever to have been rowed in those waters.

The next day was a dreary one with sunshine only at times and the wind turning slowly round the clock, but on that day we passed our 2,000-mile mark, and we celebrated with steak and kidney pie and plum pudding. With 2,000 miles gone and over 4,000 yet to go, the larder looked as well stocked as ever, and we had only finished one of our five tanks of water. In the starboard bunk in the main cabin the twice-baked bread was holding out splendidly. It was getting hard, but it was not mouldy, and it was infinitely preferable to biscuit.

The oranges were still in good condition, and it looked as if they would last for another week or two. We had our own bottled and tinned meat from the farm in Canada, and bottled venison, as well as various other brands of tinned meat and tongue. We still had some salami sausage left, and all kinds of tinned vegetables. We had our own bottled plums, and our own tinned pears and apples. We also had tinned loganberries, strawberries, and apricots. Beryl is the most wonderful provider, and looking back on that trip, we always seemed to have been having new treats and surprises. For drinks we had any amount of grapefruit and orange juice, and the whole run of cocoa, chocolate, and Ovaltine. The eggs were still in good condition, and by great good fortune we had found some maggots in one of the sides of bacon. This had put John permanently off bacon and there was all the more for Beryl and me. We never suffered from shortage of food or drink, or from lack of variety, and our health was excellent.

The fourth week started with a fresh wind from the north. For the first few days we made good progress, sometimes close-hauled, sometimes with the wind abeam, and sometimes under twins. There was no question in this sea of the leisurely trade wind progress, day after day, with never a sail change for hundreds of miles. We were working all the time to get the best out of her, and sometimes she was hard pressed and close-hauled, under a double-reefed main and storm-jib. The 17th was one of those blustery close-hauled days, with the spray flying, and albatrosses turning into the wind to land, holding themselves for a moment quite motionless above the water, and dispensing with the tobog-ganing technique.

Clio went to school on that day. This was the life that she knew so well: the spray spattering on the deck, the glimpse of the log on the wave crest behind us and the gull dipping down to investigate it, and the never-ceasing swing and heave of the ship. She could picture in her mind what we were doing, feel the wind whip her hair as she put her head out of the hatch, imagine the urgency of our movement and the long anticipation of the landfall. We thought of her, who a few months before had been diving along the coral reef with a spear in her hand, now on her way to school in a suburban train.

The end of the week would have suited her particularly, because we were becalmed again. In the days when she was with us she used to spend hours trying to fish up the lowest forms of sea life. Now we had some strange examples drifting past us, like transparent piggy banks with two small reddish coins inside them. They collapsed into nothing if we tried to pick them out of the water, and some were joined together, end to end, to make long, and slowly writhing, transparent snakes.

The albatrosses too were particularly interesting, as today they were making their courting play. One sat opposite the other, and one would raise its wings high over its head and close together, and then give a long shrill whistle, at the same time holding its beak vertically upwards. They would then both dip their beaks in the water and offer each other drops of water and little albatrossy kisses. From then on, in reasonable weather, we often heard this wolf-whistle, and looked out to find the same procedure going on. In the evening we played 'Toto-poly', a game of racing and training horses. Altogether it was a day that Clio would have enjoyed.

On the last day of the fourth week, John awoke me to say that the wind was round in the south-east and that we were heading north-west. We dropped the twins and set all sail and then started striding along again—a great relief after making only seventy miles in the past three days. The predatory skua was round again, and attacked an albatross, which squawked and landed in the water. Also a beautiful mothlike little petrel of a light dove-grey and with a black cap. At six in the evening we were becalmed after doing forty-seven miles in exactly six hours, and we were left rolling about in the most confused sea imaginable with the tops falling backwards off the waves, and dark lowering clouds all around. The glass was falling, all order had gone from the sea, and there was an eerie feeling about in this strange, jagged moonscape of a deserted ocean. We brought down the sails, and soon after supper we turned in.

Early in the morning we woke to hear a sail flogging the deck wildly. We scrambled out and found a bitter wind blowing freshly from the north-east. We made the sail fast.

'Variable Westerlies.'

'No, the Variables are between the Westerlies and the Trades,' said John.

'Anyway, these aren't variables, they're constants, and they're Easterlies.'

We grumbled our way back into our bunks again.

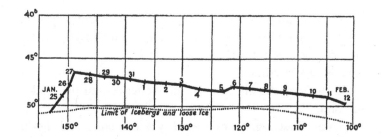

CHAPTER SIX

THE WAY OF A SHIP

THE wind was still in the east in the morning, and we decided to change our tactics and to search for more favourable winds in slightly lower latitudes. Under double-reefed main and storm-jib, with low rain clouds driving across her bow, and the bottom of her sails wet with spray, *Tzu Hang* strained to the north. For the next three days the wind was blowing from the east, and it was blowing hard. For a part of the time it was blowing force 8 and we were reduced to a storm headsail only, but at other times we made good progress. At any rate we kept going, and we felt proud of the way in which she was buffeting through a stiff uncomfortable sea. She seemed to relish the struggle, and we had immense confidence in her. For over three weeks now we had been south of latitude 50° south, which was, as far as we knew, a lot further south than the track of any other yacht that had crossed the South Pacific before us.

There were not many that we knew of, which had been bound direct for the Straits of Magellan or the Horn. Only *Saoirse*,

70

Pandora, and *Waltzing Matilda*. All of them had sailed from Auckland and so their tracks, for most of the way, had been a long way north of ours. *Saoirse*, when she finally made her run down for the Horn, had rounded it in perfect weather, and went on to complete her passage to England. *Pandora* rounded the Horn, and was nearly lost in a gale south of the Falkland Islands, and was picked up by a steamer, after being rolled completely over. *Waltzing Matilda*, on her wonderful passage to England, entered the Patagonian Channels, in the Golfo de Peñas, in latitude 47° and thereafter was in comparatively sheltered water. Vito Dumas, of the Argentine, who sailed round the world during the war, in the forties, went from New Zealand to Valparaiso and then round the Horn and up to Buenos Aires; an astounding single-handed trip.

There are not many yachts of comparable size that have been down in Patagonian waters at all. Captain Slocum, the first single-handed circumnavigator, who has inspired all single-handers ever since, sailed from east to west through the Straits of Magellan, and then was driven south. He escaped back into the Channels through Cockburn Passage, known as the Milky Way, because of the breaking white water all along on its many dangers. Then there was Al Hansen who sailed through the Straits and up through the Channels in 1934, but was lost on the coast of Chiloe, on his way north. Since the war Bardiaux sailed his *Les Quatre Vents* through the Straits of Le Maire, where he was rolled clean over twice, without being dismasted, and then round the Horn and back into the Beagle Channel, and while we were still in the Southern Ocean, a mountaineer and sailor, H. W. Tilman, was bringing his yacht, *Mischief*, through the Straits and up the Channels. There are of course others, which I don't know about, but I believe that *Tzu Hang* was the first small yacht to sail the old sailing ship route south of New Zealand, bound towards the Horn.

On Sunday, January 27, we were up to latitude 46° 55′, further north than we had intended to go, but it brought a change in the weather. The wind was moderating and backing. On Monday night we were becalmed; by four in the morning we were sailing again with the wind in the west, and from then on the wind stayed in the westerly quarters. In fact it did as we had expected it to do. As depression followed depression across the Southern Ocean, the wind veered to the north with a falling glass, and then backed slowly round to the south-west. To begin with we would be under fore-and-aft rig, and as the wind backed we went under twins again, and remained under them for most of the time.

The westerly winds came gently at first, with dull grey skies and a rising glass, and we marked their arrival by catching a blue codlike fish. It had large, black deep-set eyes, triangular gill-covers, and spikes on its dorsal fin.

We are often asked if we catch many fish on *Tzu Hang* and we have to admit that the number of fish that we have caught, in 30,000 miles, can be counted on the fingers of my two hands. I feel very unsporting when I have to tell of my fishing exploits, because there are virtually none. We usually trail a spoon behind, hoping that some fish, not too big, will attach itself to the lure, for the sake of the cat. Sometimes the spoon is removed, and sometimes we find the fishing line inextricably tangled with the log-line, and a half-drowned fish on the end. Our small catch has been varied. Bonito, albacore, barracuda, dolphin, and a fish called in South America a *sierra*. Most of them weighed between 16 and 20 lb., and by the time they were cut up and cooked, the whole boat, including us and the cat, stank of fish. Beryl hates wasting anything, and by the time the fish is finished everyone except the cat has had a surfeit of fish-steaks and fish-cakes, and no one is very enthusiastic about further fishing. We find also that we only catch fish on the continental shelves, or within soundings, and this blue fish was the first exception. Very good he was too, but Pwe is the only member of the crew who really thinks that fishing is worth while.

On February 1 we had been thirty-six days at sea and we had only done 3,523 miles on the chart, but we knew that we would soon catch up on our estimate of 100 miles a day, if only the winds stayed favourable. We were soon down to 48° south again, with glorious westerly weather, cold and sunny, and John was busy about the ship with his camera. He did a lot of filming from the cross-trees. Beryl and John said that they preferred the dull grey days that we had had further south, with the low driven cloud and the big swinging grey seas. A monotone, cold, powerful, and impersonal. That was what they had expected down here.

'Not the cruel sea,' Beryl said. 'The sea is impersonal. I don't see how you can call it cruel. It's the people on it who are apt to be cruel. I don't think that you would call mountains or the sea cruel. It's only that we are so small and ineffective against them, and when things go wrong we start blaming them and calling them cruel.'

'Got to blame something,' said John. 'You never get anywhere blaming yourself.'

'No, I think that it's jolly hard luck on them. I think that they are kind, both the mountains and the sea, and it's only that they are so big that they don't notice us, or seem to forget about us.'

'I thought that you said that they were impersonal.'

'Well, impersonal in that they don't feel spite against us. We are just so small that they don't notice us.'

'Didn't Hillary say, after he had climbed Everest, that he felt as if the mountain had sort of noticed them, and given them permission? Same sort of thing in reverse.'

'Yes, I don't think that anyone should ever mention victory or conquest with regard to the sea or the mountains. I think that you can talk about a fight or a struggle, in the same way as an ant could talk about struggling up your trousers, but I don't think that it could talk of victory, when it got to the top.'

'You wouldn't like the sea if there wasn't an almost continual struggle,' I said, and then to John: 'Life with Beryl has been one long struggle for survival. The army ought to hire her to run a battle course for the next war.'

'No wonder you look your age.'

'I once had a confidential report which said, "This Officer shows great skill in getting out of situations he should never have got into." It should have been "getting out of situations his wife has got him into".'

Beryl and John might prefer the grey smoking seas, but I liked this sun and movement, this sparkle on the water, the blues and the greens, the dazzle and flash of the spray at the bow, and the small white clouds.

For three days the wind stayed fresh in the west, and never had we had such sailing. The stove was kept on all day and it was warm and snug in the cabin, and on deck *Tzu Hang* seemed to be singing a wild saga of high adventure. The big swells built up, showing a greenish blue at their tops against the sky and as they rolled up from behind, *Tzu Hang* leaped forward in a flurry of foam, weaving, swaying, and surging, in an ecstasy of movement and sun and spray.

She seemed such a valiant little ship to us; so strong, so competent, so undismayed; so entirely ready to deal with anything that the wind might bring. As we walked around her, feeling the shrouds, checking the shackles, and tallowing the sheets, we felt that there was nothing there now that could let us down. We seemed to know every part of her: her weaknesses and her strengths.

Her mainmast was new. John had made it for us in the Hawaiian Islands out of clear Oregon pine. It was fibre-glassed all over, and you could see the grain through the fibre-glass, without a knot or a glue-line showing. The mizzenmast we had overhauled and fibre-glassed in Sydney. It was as good as new, and we had made a new main boom in Auckland. Her rigging was all of stainless steel, and it was new, and her sheets and halliards all of terylene. Below decks she was the same as ever, a dry boat, and I don't think that I had pumped her out more than once a week since we started, and then a few strokes only. As we sat below, we could hear no complaint from her. Only the noises that we knew so well: the happy noises of a good ship sailing well. However wild it was outside, there was an impression of home and comfort down below. Now that we had the fire going all the time, everything was dry and warm. The kettle on the fire, the cat, the knitting, the rows of books, and the made-up bunks, gave a feeling of well-being and security not altogether in keeping with the conditions outside. The jersey was growing, and Beryl had got to the stage of measuring it against John's large, and apparently expanding, front. John was engaged in making a pair of parallel rules out of copper and perspex.

We had two radio sets on board, as John had brought his with him from *Trekka*. I had a Hallicraft and John had a Zenith Trans-Oceanic, both dry battery sets. We had fixed John's close up under the deck and above the stove. Some dampness had got inside, and it was inclined to be temperamental. Now that it was in a warm dry place it began to function perfectly again, so that with two radio sets working, we could afford to listen to the B.B.C. programmes, and we got very good reception on the South American service. We relied on the B.B.C. for our time signal, for we could not get the WWV American station, our usual stand-by. Radio Moscow was also inevitably on the air, and we began to pick up 'The Voice of the Andes', the first sign, other than the row of crosses on the chart, that we were approaching our destination.

The South Pacific is covered by two Admiralty charts, from Port Phillip Bay to Cape Buen Suceso, in the Straits of Le Maire, the final tip of Tierra del Fuego. We folded the charts in two, so that they would fit better on the chart-table, and the daily positions, as we plotted them, stretched slowly across successive halves. We were now well across the first half of the second chart. On this half there was only one small piece of land, Easter Island, which squeezed into the margin, in the top corner. When we turned the chart over, the Patagonian coast would be in sight on the chart, if not in fact, and we would be able to plot our course down to the Diego Ramirez Islands, which we hoped to make our landfall for the Horn.

On February 5 the wind went round to the north-west, and the glass began to fall. Next day it was down to 29·25, and blowing a gale force from the west. The twins were fluttering at their peaks, making a purring sound, and sometimes snapping loudly. They only do this at about force 8, and it is really time to take them down then. We took them in in the afternoon and went on under a storm-jib only. We had to keep watch and steer under this rig, and we rigged a canvas windbreak round the stem to give the helmsman some shelter. It was a great improvement.

Conditions were so bad on deck that we cut the watches down to two-hour shifts, and found them about one hour and forty-five minutes too long. At four in the morning we hauled the jib in taut and let *Tzu Hang* go by herself, with the helm lashed amidships, and at seven we set the twins again.

The first day of the seventh week, with the wind strong in the south-west, we made great progress, although a little too much to the north, and the second day the same, so that in the afternoon we changed to fore-and-aft sails to correct our course, and sailed like this all through the night, and in the morning we set the twins again. We had a great struggle to get them up as it was blowing force 7 at least. The next two days were splendid sailing with the wind fresh in the west, and on one of them we listened to the England *v.* Ireland Rugby match on the B.B.C.

On the 11th, forty-seven days out, we had 4,749 miles on the log, and from now on we hoped to improve on the average of 100 miles a day. We thought that we had had all the calm weather and contrary winds for this passage. But it was a dull day, with little wind, and John persuaded us to launch the dinghy again, on the end of the sixty fathoms of manilla rope that we had in the stern. We put it over, with John and his camera inside, and it looked horribly perilous. The dinghy kept riding up on the swell, so that it seemed as if it was going to overtake us, and when we brought it up to the yacht again, it looked for a moment as if it was going to come on board by itself. John filmed away, quite oblivious of any danger.

'I hope I've got your two frightened faces,' he said.

'It was only the camera we were frightened about. We couldn't lose you if we tried.'

One morning I found a squid in the cockpit. Pwe ate it, but I thought that the ink sac might be too rich for her and make her sick. I threw it overboard. Perhaps she thought that this was the choicest piece, and was keeping it till last, because she was very angry about it.

The day after John's filming, the glass began to fall again, and the wind to veer in the usual sequence. Another depression was on its way. We had no means of telling how big. We were the weather ship. We continued under twins, but during the night I found that we were running south-east, and an hour later due south. We turned out and set the double-reefed main, staysail, and storm-jib. At 09.00 the wind was backing so we set the twins again, but the glass was still dropping, and it was blowing gale force with a big following sea. We were well on to the last quarter of the second chart.

The twins began to flutter again in the afternoon, and we managed to harden them down to stop it. The sea was most awe-inspiring, a bigger swell than we had ever seen and wide breaking crests. It was better on deck than below, because on deck we could see *Tzu Hang* riding so buoyantly, tearing away on her course, her self-steering working so much better than we could steer. Below, the noise of the wind was alarming, and the glass was falling still. I went into the forecabin and saw something rolling about on the floor. 'Blue Bear has lost his head,' I shouted back to Beryl, picking it up.

'Let's throw him overboard, he's just taking up room.'

'Good heavens, no, he's our mascot.' I placed his head under his arm, where he was sitting right in the bow, on the shelf. Beryl was pouring tea into our mugs and handing them to us. She put the teapot back on to the stove, where it would not upset because of the gimbals. Outside the wind gave a long 'whoooo' in the rigging, and there was the roar of a breaking top, and a rush of water along the deck.

'Listen to that,' I said. 'The old girl's really stepping out.'

'Treats tonight,' said John, '5,000-mile plum pud.'

'No, it's fourth quarter of the chart plum pud. 5,000-mile treats tomorrow.'

Beryl gave us some oatmeal cakes that she had made for tea and we had our plum pudding that night. 'If we go on like this we'll be in Port Stanley in time to send a cable to Clio for her birthday.'

'Now you've done it. Aren't you awful,' said Beryl.

'No, not me. John's the man. He keeps asking for big waves. Won't these do you John?'

'These are all right, but I expected to see something bigger. Something like *Coimbra* had. However, I'm quite happy with these provided we get there.'

'What happened to *Coimbra*?'

'She was rolled right over in the South Atlantic, but I think that she was hove to. They lost one man off the deck. Never picked him up, but got to Tristan da Cunha, where she was finally lost while they were ashore. I think that one of them described the waves as 90 feet high, and the top 30 breaking.'

'Hell, we don't want to see anything like that.'

We were running fast, and the motion was violent, and I was anxious, but I wanted to hold on as long as I could.

CHAPTER SEVEN

THIS IS SURVIVAL TRAINING!

It must have been nearly five in the morning, because it was light again, when the noise of the headsails became so insistent that I decided to take in sail. I pulled on my boots and trousers. Now that I had decided to take some action I felt that it was already late, and was in a fever to get on with it. When I was dressed I slid back the hatch, and the wind raised its voice in a screech as I did so. In the last hour there had been an increase in the wind, and the spindrift was lifting, and driving across the face of the sea.

I shut the hatch and went forward to call Beryl. She was awake, and when I went aft to call John, he was awake also. They both came into the doghouse to put on their oilies. As we got dressed there was a feeling that this was something unusual; it was rather like a patrol getting ready to leave, with the enemy in close contact. In a few minutes we were going to be struggling with this gale and this furious-looking sea, but for the time being we were safe and in shelter.

'Got your life-lines?' Beryl asked.

'No, where the hell's my life-line? It was hanging up with the oilies.' Like my reading glasses, it was always missing.

'Here it is,' John said. He was buckling on a thick leather belt over his jacket, to which his knife, shackle spanner, and life-line were attached. His life-line was a thin nylon cord with a snap-hook at the end, and Beryl's, incongruously, was a thick terylene rope, with a breaking strain of well over a ton.

'Got the shackle spanner?' I asked. 'Never mind, here's a wrench. Is the forehatch open?' Someone said that they'd opened it.

'Beryl, take the tiller. John and I'll douse the sails. Come on boys, into battle.' I slid the hatch back again and we climbed up one after the other. We were just on the crest of a wave and could look around over a wide area of stormy greyish-white sea. Because we were on the top of a wave for a moment, the seas did not look too bad, but the wind rose in a high pitched howl, and plucked at the double shoulders of our oilies, making the flaps blow up and down.

The wave passed under *Tzu Hang*. Her bowsprit rose, and she gave a waddle and lift as if to say, 'Be off with you!' Then the sea broke, and we could hear it grumbling away ahead of us, leaving a great wide band of foam behind it.

Beryl slipped into the cockpit and snapped her life-line on to the shrouds. John and I went forward, and as we let go of the handrail on the doghouse, we snapped the hooks of our life-lines on to the rail, and let them run along the wire until we had hold of the shrouds. The wind gave us a push from behind as we moved. I went to the starboard halliard and John to the port, and I looked aft to see if Beryl was ready. Then we unfastened the poles from the mast and let the halliards go, so that the sails came down together, and in a very short time we had them secured. We unhooked them from the stays, bundled them both down the forehatch, and secured the two booms to the rails. As we went back to the cockpit, we were bent against the pitch of the ship and the wind. Beryl unfastened the sheets from the tiller and we coiled them up and threw them below.

'How's she steering?'

'She seems to steer all right, I can steer all right.'

'We'll let the stern-line go anyway, it may be some help.'

John and I uncoiled the 3-inch hawser, which was lashed in the stern, and paid it out aft. Then we took in the log-line, in case it should be fouled by the hawser. By the time everything was finished, my watch was nearly due, so I took over the tiller from Beryl, and the others went below. The hatch slammed shut, and I was left to myself. I turned my attention to the sea.

The sea was a wonderful sight. It was as different from an ordinary rough sea, as a winter's landscape is from a summer one, and the thing that impressed me most was that its general aspect was white. This was due to two reasons: firstly because the wide breaking crests left swathes of white all over the sea, and secondly because all over the surface of the great waves themselves, the wind was whipping up lesser waves, and blowing their tops away, so that the whole sea was lined and streaked with this blown spume, and it looked as if all the surface was moving. Here and there, as a wave broke, I could see the flung spray caught and whirled upwards by the wind, which raced up the back of the wave, just like a whirl of wind-driven sand in the desert. I had seen it before, but this moving surface, driving low across a sea all lined and furrowed with white, this was something new to me, and something frightening, and I felt exhilarated with the atmosphere of strife. I have felt this feeling before on a mountain, or in battle, and I should have been warned. It is apt to mean trouble.

For the first time since we entered the Tasman there were no albatrosses to be seen. I wondered where they had gone to, and supposed that however hard the wind blew it could make no

82

difference to them. Perhaps they side-slipped out of a storm area, or perhaps they held their position as best they could until the storm passed, gliding into the wind and yet riding with the storm until it left them.

I kept looking aft to make sure that *Tzu Hang* was dead stem on to the waves. First her stem lifted, and it looked as if we were sliding down a long slope into the deep valley between this wave and the one that had passed, perhaps twenty seconds before; then for a moment we were perched on the top of a sea, the wind force rose, and I could see the white desolation around me. Then her bowsprit drove into the sky, and with a lurch and a shrug, she sent another sea on its way. It was difficult to estimate her speed, because we had brought the log in, and the state of the water was very disturbed, but these waves were travelling a great deal faster than she was, and her speed seemed to be just sufficient to give her adequate steerage way, so that I could correct her in time to meet the following wave.

Suddenly there was a roar behind me and a mass of white water foamed over the stern. I was knocked forward out of the cockpit on to the bridge deck, and for a moment I seemed to be sitting in the sea with the mizzenmast sticking out of it upright beside me. I was surprised by the weight of the water, which had burst the canvas windscreen behind me wide open, but I was safely secured by my life-line to the after shroud. I scrambled back into the cockpit and grabbed the tiller again, and pushed it hard over, for *Tzu Hang* had swung so that her quarter was to the sea. She answered slowly but in time, and as the next sea came up, we were stern on to it again. The canvas of the broken windscreen lashed and fluttered in the wind until its torn ends were blown away.

Now the cloud began to break up and the sun to show. I couldn't look at the glass, but I thought that I felt the beginning of a change.

It was only the change of some sunlight, but the sunlight seemed to show that we were reaching the bottom of this depression. Perhaps we would never get a chance again to film such a sea, in these fleeting patches of brilliance. I beat on the deck above John's bunk and called him up. I think that he had just got to sleep, now that the sails were off her, and there was someone at the helm. I know that I couldn't sleep before. He looked sleepy and disgruntled when he put his head out of the hatch.

'What about some filming, John?'

'No, man, the sea never comes out.'

'We may never get a sea like this again.'

'I don't want to get the camera wet, and there's not enough light.'

'No, look, there's a bit of sun about.'

As he was grumbling, like an old bear roused out of its winter quarters, he looked aft and I saw his expression change to one of interest.

'Look at this one coming up,' he said, peering over the top of the washboards, just the top of his head and his eyes showing. 'Up she goes,' he ducked down as if he expected some spray to come over, and then popped his head up again. 'Wait a minute,' he said, 'I'll fix something up,' and he slammed the hatch shut and disappeared below again.

He came up in a few minutes, fully equipped. He had the camera in a plastic bag with the lens protruding through a small hole. He took some shots. The lens had to be dried repeatedly, but the camera was safe in its bag, and we had no more wave tops on board. Presently he went down again.

John relieved me for breakfast, and when I came up it seemed to be blowing harder than ever.

'How's she steering?' I asked him.

'Not bad,' he said. 'I think she's a bit sluggish, but she ought to do.'

I took over again, and he went below; no one wanted to hang about in this wind. I watched the sixty fathoms of 3-inch hawser streaming behind. It didn't seem to be making a damn of difference, although I suppose that it was helping to keep her stern on to the seas. Sometimes I could see the end being carried forward in a big bight on the top of a wave. We had another sixty fathoms, and I considered fastening it to the other and streaming the two in a loop, but I had done this before, and the loop made no difference, although the extra length did help to slow her down. We had oil on board, but I didn't consider the emergency warranted the use of oil. For four hours now we had been running before this gale, running in the right direction, and we had only had one breaking top on board, and although I had been washed away from the tiller, *Tzu Hang* had shown little tendency to broach to. To stop her and to lie a-hull in this big sea seemed more dangerous than to let her run, as we were doing now. It was a dangerous sea I knew, but I had no doubt that she would carry us safely through, and as one great wave after another rushed past us, I grew more and more confident.

Beryl relieved me at nine o'clock. She looked so gay when she came on deck, for this is the sort of thing that she loves. She was wearing her yellow oilskin trousers and a yellow jumper with a hood, and over all a green oilskin coat. So that she could put on enough pairs of socks, she was wearing a spare pair of John's sea-boots. She was wearing woollen gloves, and she had put a plastic bag over her left hand, which she wouldn't be using for the tiller. She snapped the shackle of her life-line on to the shroud, and sat down beside me, and after a minute or two she took over. I went below to look at the glass and saw that it had moved up a fraction. My camera was in the locker in the doghouse, and I brought it out and took some snaps of the sea. Beryl was concentrating very hard on the steering. She was looking at the compass, and then aft to the following sea, to make sure that she was stern on to it, and then back to the compass again, but until she had the feel of the ship she would trust more to the compass for her course than to the wind and the waves. I took one or two snaps of Beryl, telling her not to look so serious, and to give me a smile. She laughed at me.

'How do you think she's steering?'

'Very well, I think.'

'We could put the other line out. Do you think she needs it? The glass is up a bit.'

'No, I think she's all right.'

'Sure you're all right?'

'Yes, fine, thanks.'

I didn't want to leave her and to shut the hatch on her, and cut her off from us below, but we couldn't leave the hatch open, and there was no point in two of us staying on deck. I took off my oilskins, put the camera back in its plastic bag in the locker, and climbed up into my bunk. The cat joined me and sat on my stomach. She swayed to the roll and purred. I pulled my book out of the shelf and began to read. After a time, I heard John open the hatch again and start talking to Beryl. A little later he went up to do some more filming. As the hatch opened there was a roar from outside, but *Tzu Hang* ran on straight and true, and I felt a surge of affection and pride for the way she was doing. 'She's a good little ship, a good little ship,' I said to her aloud, and patted her planking.

I heard the hatch slam shut again, and John came down. He went aft, still dressed in his oilskins, and sat on the locker by his bunk, changing the film of his camera. Beneath him, and lashed securely to ring-bolts on the locker, was his tool-box, a large wooden chest, about 30 inches by 18 inches by 8 inches, crammed full with heavy tools.

My book was called *Harry Black*, and Harry Black was following up a wounded tiger, but I never found out what happened to Harry Black and the tiger.

When John went below, Beryl continued to steer as before, continually checking her course by the compass, but steering more by the wind and the waves. She was getting used to them now, but the wind still blew as hard as ever. In places the sun broke through the cloud, and from time to time she was in sunshine. A wave passed under *Tzu Hang*, and she slewed slightly. Beryl corrected her easily, and when she was down in the hollow she looked aft to check her alignment. Close behind her a great wall of water was towering above her, so wide that she couldn't see its flanks, so high and so steep that she knew *Tzu Hang* could not ride over it. It didn't seem to be breaking as the other waves had broken, but water was cascading down its front, like a waterfall. She thought, 'I can't do anything, I'm absolutely straight.' This was her last visual picture, so nearly truly her last, and it has remained with her. The next moment she seemed to be falling out of the cockpit, but she remembers nothing but this sensation. Then she found herself floating in the sea, unaware whether she had been under water or not.

She could see no sign of *Tzu Hang*, and she grabbed at her waist for her life-line, but felt only a broken end. She kicked to tread water, thinking, 'Oh, God, they've left me!' and her boots, those good roomy boots of John's, came off as she kicked. Then a wave lifted her, and she turned in the water, and there was *Tzu Hang*, faithful *Tzu Hang*, lying stopped and thirty yards away. She saw that the masts were gone and that *Tzu Hang* was strangely low in the water, but she was still afloat and Beryl started to swim towards the wreckage of the mizzenmast.

As I read, there was a sudden, sickening sense of disaster. I felt a great lurch and heel, and a thunder of sound filled my ears. I was conscious, in a terrified moment, of being driven into the front and side of my bunk with tremendous force. At the same time there was a tearing cracking sound, as if *Tzu Hang* was being ripped apart, and water burst solidly, raging into the cabin. There was darkness, black darkness, and pressure, and a feeling of being buried in a debris of boards, and I fought wildly to get out, thinking *Tzu Hang* had already gone. Then suddenly I was standing again, waist deep in water, and floorboards and cushions, mattresses and books, were sloshing in wild confusion round me.

I knew that some tremendous force had taken us and thrown us like a toy, and had engulfed us in its black maw. I knew that no one on deck could have survived the fury of its strength, and I knew that Beryl was fastened to the shrouds by her life-line, and could not have been thrown clear. I struggled aft, fearing what I expected to see, fearing that I would not see her alive again. As I went I heard an agonised yell from the cat, and thought, 'Poor thing, I cannot help you now.' When I am angry, or stupid and spoilt, or struggling and in danger, or in distress, there is a part of me which seems to disengage from my body, and to survey the scene with a cynical distaste. Now that I was afraid, this other half seemed to see myself struggling through all the floating debris, and to hear a distraught voice crying, 'Oh God, where's Beryl, where's Beryl?'

As I entered the galley, John's head and shoulders broke water by the galley stove. They may have broken water already, but that was my impression anyway. John himself doesn't know how he got there, but he remembers being thrown forward from where he was sitting and to port, against the engine exhaust and the petrol tank. He remembers struggling against the tremendous force of water in the darkness, and wondering how far *Tzu Hang* had gone down and whether she could ever get up again. As I passed him he got to his feet. He looked sullen and obstinate, as he might look if someone had offended him, but he said nothing. There was no doghouse left. The corner posts had been torn from the bolts in the carlins, and the whole doghouse sheared off flush with the deck. Only a great gaping square hole in the deck remained.

As I reached the deck, I saw Beryl. She was thirty yards away on the port quarter on the back of a wave, and for the moment above us, and she was swimming with her head well out of the water. She looked unafraid, and I believe that she was smiling.

'I'm all right, I'm all right,' she shouted.

I understood her although I could not hear the words, which were taken by the wind.

The mizzenmast was in several pieces, and was floating between her and the ship, still attached to its rigging, and I saw that she would soon have hold of it. When she got there, she pulled herself in on the shrouds, and I got hold of her hand. I saw that her head was bleeding, and I was able to see that the cut was not too serious but when I tried to pull her on board, although we had little freeboard left, I couldn't do it because of the weight of her sodden clothes and because she seemed to be unable to help with her other arm. I saw John standing amidships. Incredibly he was standing, because, as I could see now, both masts had gone, and the motion was now so quick that I could not keep my feet on the deck. He was standing with his legs wide apart, his knees bent and his hands on his thighs. I called to him to give me a hand. He came up and knelt down beside me, and said, 'This is it, you know, Miles.'

But before he could get hold of Beryl, he saw another wave coming up, and said, 'Look out, this really is it!'

Beryl called, 'Let go, let go!'

But I wasn't going to let go of that hand, now that I had got it, and miraculously *Tzu Hang*, although she seemed to tremble with the effort, rode another big wave. She was dispirited and listless, but she still floated. Next moment John caught Beryl by the arm, and we hauled her on board. She lay on the deck for a moment, and then said, 'Get off my arm John, I can't get up.'

'But I'm not on your arm,' he replied.

'You're kneeling on my arm, John.'

'Here,' he said, and gave her a lift up. Then we all turned on our hands and knees, and held on to the edge of the big hole in the deck.

Up to now my one idea had been to get Beryl back on board, with what intent I do not really know, because there was so much water below that I was sure *Tzu Hang* could not float much longer. I had no idea that we could save her, nor, John told me afterwards, had he. In fact, he said, the reason why he had not come at once to get Beryl on board again, was that he thought *Tzu Hang* would go before we did so. After this first action, I went through a blank patch, thinking that it was only a few moments, a few minutes of waiting, thinking despondently that I had let Clio down. Beryl's bright, unquenchable spirit thought of no such thing. 'I know where the buckets are,' she said. 'I'll get them!'

This set us working to save *Tzu Hang*.

Beryl slipped below, followed by John, but for the time being I stayed on deck and turned to look at the ruins that had been *Tzu Hang*. The tiller, the cockpit coaming, and every scrap of the doghouse had gone, leaving a 6 foot by 6 foot gap in the deck. Both masts had been taken off level with the deck, the dinghies had gone, and the cabin skylights were sheared off a few inches above the deck. The bowsprit had been broken in two. The rail stanchions were bent all over the place, and the wire was broken. A tangle of wire shrouds lay across the deck, and in the water to leeward floated the broken masts and booms—the masts broken in several places. The compass had gone, and so had the anchor which had been lashed to the foredeck.

There could be no more desolate picture. The low-lying, water-logged, helpless hull, the broken spars and wreckage, that greyish-white sea; no bird, no ship, nothing to help, except that which we had within ourselves. Now the sun was gone again, the spindrift still blew chill across the deck, and the water lipped on to it, and poured into the open hull.

I think both John and I had been numbed with shock, but he recovered first and was working in a fury now, and a hanging cupboard door, some floorboards, and the Genoa erupted on to the deck. I hung on to them, so that they would not be blown or washed off, while he went down again for his tools. He found his tool-box jammed in the sink, and when he groped under water for the tin of galvanized nails in the paint locker, he found them on his second dip. I had intended to help John, as the first essential seemed to be to get the hole covered up, but he was working so fast, so sure now of what he was going to do, his mouth set in a grim determination, oblivious of anything but the work in hand, that I saw he would do as well without me, and now Beryl, who was trying to bale, found that she could not raise the bucket to empty it. I climbed down to where Beryl was standing on the engine, the water washing about her knees. We had to feel for some foothold on the floor-bearers because the engine cover had gone. A 70-lb. keg of waterlogged flour floated up to us.

'Overboard with it,' I said.

'Mind your back,' said Beryl, as if we were working on the farm.

I picked it up, and heaved it on deck, Beryl helping with her good arm, but it seemed light enough, and John toppled it over into the sea, out of his way. Anything to lighten the ship, for she was desperately heavy and low in the water.

'We'd better bale through the skylight,' Beryl said, 'I'll fill the bucket, and you haul it up. We'll need a line. Here, take my life-line.' She undid her line from her waist and handed it to me, and I noticed that the snap-hook was broken. I tied it on to the handle of the plastic bucket.

We waded into the cabin feeling with our feet, because there were no floorboards to walk on. I climbed on to the bunk and put my head and shoulders through the skylight. Beryl was on the seat below with the water still round her knees. She filled the bucket and I pulled it up and emptied it, and dropped it down through the skylight again. It would have floated if she had not been there to fill it. It was the best that we could do, and although we worked fast, to begin with, we could just keep pace with the water coming in. No heavy seas broke over the ship, and when a top splashed over, I tried to fill the aperture with my body as best I could.

John was doing splendidly. He had made a skeleton roof over the hatch with the door and floorboards, and nailed it down, and he had made it higher in the middle, so that it would spill the water when the sail was nailed over. He was nailing the folded sail over it now, using pieces of wood as battens to hold it down. It was a rush job, but it had to be strong enough to hold out until the sea went down. As soon as he had finished he went to the other skylight and nailed the storm-jib over it. Beryl and I baled and baled. As the bucket filled she called 'Right!' and I hauled it up again. Her voice rang out cheerfully from below, 'Right ... Right ... Right!' and John's hammer beat a steady accompaniment. *Tzu Hang* began to rise slowly, and at first imperceptibly, in the water.

When John had finished with the skylight, he called to me to ask if he should let the rigging-screws go, so that the broken spars would act as a sea-anchor. I told him to do so, and he then went round the deck and loosened all the rigging-screws, leaving only one of the twin forestays attached to the deck. He had not much to work with, as the topmast forestay and the jibstay had gone with the mast, the forestay had smashed the deck fitting, and the other twin forestay had pulled its ring-bolt through the deck, stripping the thread on the ring-bolt. All the rigging was connected in some way or other, so now *Tzu Hang* drifted clear of her spars and then swung round, riding head to wind, on her single forestay. This forestay was attached to a mast fitting, on the broken mast, and the fitting was not equal to the strain now put on it, and it carried away. *Tzu Hang* swung away and drifted downwind, sideways to the sea, and that was the last that we saw of our tall masts, and the rigging, and the sails on the booms.

We baled and baled. We had two pumps on board, but the water that we were baling was filled with paper pulp from books and charts and labels. They would have clogged up with two strokes, and to begin with the pump handles themselves had been under water. John was now in the forecabin, standing on the bunks and baling through the skylight. Both he and Beryl were wearing the oilskins that they had been wearing when we upset, but I was still only in a jersey, and was beginning to feel very cold. I was continually wet with spray and salt water and lashed by the bitter wind, and my eyes were so encrusted and raw with salt, that I was finding it difficult to see. A broken spinnaker pole rolled off the deck, showing that *Tzu Hang* was coming out of the water again, and was getting more lively. I saw a big bird alight by it and start pecking at it, and I supposed that this was also a sign that the wind was beginning to abate. I peered through rimy eyes to try and identify it, and saw that it was a giant fulmar. It was the first and only one that we saw.

After a time I became so cold that I could no longer pull up the bucket, in spite of Beryl's encouragement from below.

'This is survival training, you know,' she said.

It was the first joke. Survival training or no, I had to go below for a rest and we called a halt, and John came back from the main cabin and we sat on the bunk for a short time. Beryl found a tin of Horlicks tablets in a locker that had not been burst open, and she pulled off one of her oilskins and gave it to me.

'Where is Pwe?' I asked. 'Anyone seen her?'

'No, but I can hear her from time to time. She's alive. We can't do anything about her now.'

We were making progress, for the top of the engine was showing above the water. There was over a foot less in the ship already, and we were getting down to the narrower parts of her hull. We went back to work, and I found that now I had some protection from the wind the strength came back to my arms and I had no further difficulty. All through the day and on into the evening we baled, with occasional breaks for rest and more Horlicks tablets. Before dark, almost twelve hours after the smash, we were down below the floor-bearers again. After some difficulty we managed to get the primus stove, recovered from the bilge, to burn with a feeble impeded flame, and we heated some soup, but Beryl wouldn't have any. Now that the struggle was over for the time being, she was in great pain from her shoulder, and she found that she couldn't put her foot to the ground into the bargain. She had injured it stumbling about in the cabin, with no floorboards. Some blood-clotted hair was stuck to her forehead. Like a wounded animal, she wanted to creep into some dark place and to sleep until she felt better.

We found a bedraggled rag of a cat, shivering and cold, in the shelf in the bow, and with her, the three of us climbed into John's bunk to try and get some warmth from each other.

'You know,' I said, 'if it hadn't been for John, I think that we wouldn't have been here now.'

'No,' he said. 'If there hadn't been three of us, we wouldn't be here now.'

'I don't know,' said Beryl. 'I think you were the man, the way you got those holes covered.'

'I think my tool-box having jammed in the sink, and finding those nails is what saved us, at least so far.'

Beryl said, 'If we get out of this, everyone will say that we broached, but we didn't. They'll say that there was a woman at the helm.'

'If they know you they'll say that's how they know we didn't broach, and anyway, we didn't: we just went wham. Let's leave it.'

'How far are we off shore, Miles?' John asked.

'About 900 miles from the entrance to Magellan I should say.'

'If we get out of this, it will be some journey. If there is a lull tomorrow, I'll fix these covers properly.'

'Get her seaworthy again, and get her cleaned up inside. I think that's the first thing to do.'

Beryl was restless with pain and couldn't sleep. In the end we went back to our own soggy bunks. As we lay, sodden and shivering, and awoke from fitful slumber to hear the thud of a wave against the side of the ship and the patter and splash of the spray on the deck, we could hear the main-sheet traveller sliding up and down on its horse. The sheet had gone with the boom, but the traveller was still there, and this annoying but familiar noise seemed to accentuate the feeling that the wreck was just a dream in spite of the water which cascaded from time to time through the makeshift covers. The old familiar noises were still there, and it was hard to believe that *Tzu Hang* was not a live ship, still running bravely down for the Horn.

For several days to come, although all our energies were spent in overcoming the difficulties of the changed situation, it seemed impossible to accept its reality.

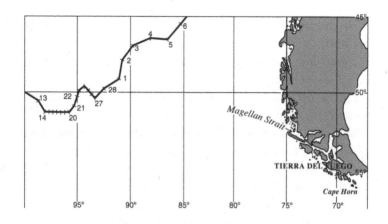

CHAPTER EIGHT

RECOVERY

WHEN daylight came to the forecabin, and percolated dimly through the sails covering the holes in the deck on to the dank jumble that lay higgledy-piggledy throughout the ship, we set about breakfast.

Beryl, as indomitable as ever, was not prepared to let either of us usurp her position in the galley. She was the first up and set to work on the primus stove. The matches we had recovered from a large watertight tin that we had kept stowed in the stern. We found spare primus prickers in a locker in the forepeak, which had also remained inviolate, and the stove was soon going again in its familiar robust manner. Tea and sugar she found somewhere in the galley shelves, or about the galley, still in their plastic containers, and we rescued a 2-gallon glass bottle of egg powder from under John's bunk. We had a dozen tins of lifeboat ration biscuits in the shelf in the forepeak, still more or less undisturbed. What a breakfast that was! As if there had been some benevolent genie in the bottle of egg powder, whom we had released to serve up life and hope and enthusiasm with the breakfast.

As we ate we planned our day. First we had to bale out the ship again, but it did begin to look now as if there was no damage to the hull. In spite of the water that had come into the ship from the deck during the night—and to our anxious imagination it seemed that tons had poured in—it was still below the floor-bearers. Next we had to make the coverings on the deck really strong and seaworthy.

'What's it like outside?' Beryl asked.

'Like the picture of "A Hopeless Dawn",' I replied.

'Do you think that you can manage?'

'Oh, yes,' said John. 'Anyway we've got to. I don't want any more nights like that with the water coming in, and wondering whether you've got to get up and bale again all the time. If I can fix the coverings properly she ought to float all right anyway.'

'I think that we must try and get the cabin stove going after that, otherwise I'm afraid that Pwe is going to pack up.'

Pwe was in very bad shape. Although Beryl had cuddled her all night, she still looked as if she had only just been pulled out of the water. She wouldn't eat and was listless and miserable. Everything that she had trusted in had gone. The security of the ship, the warmth and the comfort had vanished in a single cata-clysmic moment, and it looked as if she thought that life was no longer worth the struggle.

We uncovered one of the skylights, and baled again until we had most of the water out of the fore part of the ship. Then John and I went on deck to fix the cover over the doghouse opening. It was no longer a doghouse now, and we referred to it as the main hatch. The wind was down, but there was a wild looking sea, and the motion on deck was violent. John at times ventured on to his feet, but I moved about on my hands and knees or in a sitting position.

After taking off the Genoa, John set about improving the frame over which it was nailed. First he fastened two-by-twos, the poles from the two canvas bunks in the main cabin, round the edges of the whole opening, so that the frame would be slightly higher than the deck. Then he laid three or four floorboards, or two-by-fours, fore-and-aft across the opening, the centre ones being slightly thicker than the outside ones. Next he covered these from side to side with plywood sheeting, and nailed it down to the side pieces. The result was a slightly curved roof, just above the deck level, but our plywood was limited and there were one or two gaps in it. Over this framework we stretched the Genoa, folded three times, and we nailed it down all round with wooden battens, which we got by knocking the frames from wooden lattice window covers, which were supposed to screw into the old doghouse windows for their protection, but which we never used.

By the time we had finished, the cover to this 6 by 6 feet hole was strong enough to stand on and was absolutely waterproof. John then turned his attention to the skylights, squaring up the broken sides, building them up with plywood and nailing plywood over the top, and finally covering them with canvas. Fortunately Beryl had always been a determined hoarder, and John and I had rarely been allowed to throw away unwanted pieces of wood. Since John had joined the ship, I had been able to get rid of one or two awkward pieces, by passing them to him, and when the expert advised that they should be got rid of, she had sometimes consented. On the whole her store remained undiminished in *Tzu Hang*'s canoe stem, where all unwanted things went. Now all kinds of old favourites, condemned and reprieved, were brought to light and made use of.

I left John with the skylights and went below again to dig in the mass of tins and paper pulp for the stove tops; the cabin stove had four tops and all were missing. They had left some marks on the deckhead above to show that they had been about during the smash. Amongst the debris we found a complete, heavy, bronze porthole, knocked out of the front of the doghouse, lying in the bilge by the galley. Its partner, also complete, we found in John's cabin. The starboard doorpost of this after-cabin had been smashed by John's tool-box, in its flight to the sink, after breaking away from its lashings, and it now seemed that while John and his tool-box were on their way out, the heavy porthole had been on its way in. As the other port was lying where I had first seen John as he emerged from the water, he must have been just missed by both barrels. Lying on its side in the rubbish in the main cabin was the sewing machine. We threw it and the ports overboard. We tended to throw all kinds of things over the side in a kind of desperation induced by the devastation below. Many things we might have made use of or restored later on, but we were still none too sure that we had a future.

Wedged down in the bilge of the forecabin was the headless corpse of Blue Bear.

'Here's that bloody Blue Bear,' I said. 'I'm going to throw him overboard.'

'Poor Blue Bear,' said Beryl, thinking for a moment of Clio, 'I suppose he'd better go.'

'He hasn't been much use to us, has he?'

'Well, he must have his head too.'

We found his head and put him, not ungently, into the sea, and I expect the albatrosses pulled the straw out of his tight blue tummy and picked out his button black eyes before he sank.

While the ship had been so full of water, she had been acting as a kind of gigantic Mixmaster to all the stores inside her. Most of the lockers could be got at from the top, and during *Tzu Hang*'s cartwheel, or whatever antics she had gone through, they had emptied their contents into the cabin. All the tins lay piled in the bilges and all their paper covers had come off. There was paper pulp everywhere from labels and books and charts. It looked like the output of a pulp mill. Mixed in with it was broken glass, marmalade, bottled meat no longer in bottles, seventy broken eggs, soggy lumps of twice-baked bread, ashes and coke. The whole was tied together with glutinous tendons from skeins and skeins of coloured wool, which had been going into John's jersey, and which were destined for several other jerseys that Beryl had hoped to make during the voyage, as a sideline to her many other activities. But not only wool. Marline, fishing line, caulking cotton and fish-hooks all helped to bind it together. This mess was topped off by odd clothing, soaking Dunlopillo cushions and seats, and out-of-place floorboards. Almost everything that could be needed in a yacht equipped for long-distance cruising for a year was there, even if it couldn't be found.

We had no particular wish—nor the time so far—to discuss what had happened to *Tzu Hang*, but as we worked we began to notice all kinds of things that helped us to put together our incoherent impressions. Some of the drawers in the forecabin, which had not fallen out of their places, had nevertheless emptied their contents to mix with the muddle in the bilge. After digging away vigorously for several hours, and emptying bucket after bucket of rubbish over the side, we found the last of the stove lids. We couldn't find the hatchet, but we set to work splitting wet wood with a knife, until we got sufficient dry shavings. Beryl gave them a liberal douche of kerosene and, after a major explosion, we had a fire. During the afternoon she had been persuaded to lie down, and we doped her with pain-killer and sleeping pills, and she awoke feeling rather better. Now she appointed herself mistress of the stove as well as the galley.

The chimney had gone with everything else on the deck and, as *Tzu Hang* rose on a wave, the smoke billowed out of every corner of the stove, and spread throughout the ship. It seemed to hang about from the deckhead down to about knee height. For the next few days, when Beryl was not sitting on the cabin floor sorting out the mess, she sat crouched over the cabin stove, trying to coax the fire into flame. She looked for all the world like an old witch, who had escaped to her cave from the fury of the mob. Her hair, still clotted with dried blood, stuck to her forehead, her face was blackened with soot, and a starved-looking cat trembled on her lap. The smoke eddied round her, and when John and I, her two minions, entered the cabin, we came in crouched in obeisance, in our efforts to keep below smoke level, and coughing apologetically. Beryl, witchlike, remained impervious to the fumes, but here the likeness ended, for her enthusiasm seemed to sparkle through the cabin, bringing light even to its drab darkness.

We did need some more light in the cabin, because now that the skylights and the main hatch were boarded up, it was very dark below. John decided that he'd put perspex lights in both of them when he had the opportunity.

That night Beryl and I slept on the floor of the cabin, while John wedged himself in a seat and attempted to keep warm by keeping the stove alight. We drugged Beryl again and she slept fairly well, after wedging herself with wet pillows. As a result of the first day's work we felt that we were now safe enough so far as keeping afloat was concerned, and we were able to take a look at the balance sheet. We were about 900 miles west of the entrance to the Straits of Magellan. We had plenty of food, and we still had water, with reasonable rationing, for 100 days, and could devise something to catch more if necessary. If we were unable to sail, the drift of the current would take us round the Horn, unless we were first set on shore by westerly or south-westerly winds, and once round the Horn, the Falkland current would take us up towards the Falklands. If we got to the Falklands, Port Stanley was right at the leeward, the eastern end, and it would entail a turn to windward to make it, and if we missed it and were not seen, the next stop would be Africa. Anyway the Falklands were no place to approach under jury-rig if it could be avoided. We decided that we must keep the land to leeward so that in the end we could make land somewhere, but that we must try to get up north to warmer seas and calmer latitudes, out of the Cape Horn current and into the northerly drift, so that we would have a reasonable chance of making a port.

We had a skilled carpenter on board, we had all the tools and the wood and the screws to build a mast, and we had spare wire and rope and sails. If Beryl got better, and our health stayed all right, there was no reason why we shouldn't make it. Half the things we wanted were still mixed with the paper pulp in the bilges, but they were there.

We had other assets too. My radio set had been completely immersed, and we couldn't get a kick out of it, but John's, screwed up under the deckhead amidships, had escaped a serious ducking, although stuck to the deckhead only two feet from it was a wad of wet ashes from the stove. Now, when we tested John's set, warmed by the stove below it, we found that it worked. Our navigational books, wedged tight in their shelves, had survived, and the sextants were all right. The chronometer, with some water showing under its glass, was still running. No single chart had survived, but we had the *American Pilot* for the west coast of South America, and we had the *National Geographic* map of the Pacific, printed on some special waterproof fabric, which had survived intact. We also found a small portion of the south-west corner of the chart of the South Atlantic which had the coast of Chile on it, or at least a portion of it, on a very small scale.

I suppose that night we may have felt rather lonely down there in those wild wastes, but we knew that it was up to us and nobody else to get ourselves out of these difficulties, and there was a feeling of companionship between the three of us in a very real adventure.

Next morning, Saturday, John decided that he would have no more nights like the last, and he was looking rather the worse for his vigil by the stove. The forecabin seemed to be going to be the first to dry out, so he transferred the canvas from his bunk aft to the starboard berth in the forecabin. The bunkboards of this berth had been used in repairs, and he nailed the canvas across it in a form of hammock. His berth aft was dark and dripping with condensation, and was too far away from the forehatch, which was the only way that we could get on deck. From then on he and I slept in the forecabin and Beryl on the floor of the main cabin. She found this the most comfortable position, between a seat and the brass pipe which held the sliding table. But we were very worried about her. For the time being her ankle was giving her more pain than her shoulder. We had bandaged it up, and now when we removed the bandage, bloodblisters began to break out all round it. Beryl's great cry with regard to sickness is that 'the tendency in nature is towards cure', and everything must be left alone as far as possible, so we were not allowed to do anything very much to help or hinder the process of repair. I gave her some penicillin in case any of these internal injuries should become inflamed, and she submitted to this without protest.

It was a mild day, and we tried to dry out one or two mattresses on the deck, but they came down wetter than when they went up. John was able to put a perspex light, neatly finished and caulked, in one of the main cabin skylights. While I was on deck, I remembered that I had heard no sound from the rudder, which should have been swinging free. We had noticed that the tiller had gone, but when I looked aft I saw that the bronze octagonal nut which held the tiller in position on the post was still there. The bronze tiller fitting must have broken wide open, but what really caught my attention was that the top of the rudder-post wasn't moving. We had fixed up the life-lines after a fashion, and now we were beginning to find our feet again on the deck. Half walking and half crawling, I made my way aft as quickly as I could, got into the cockpit, and peered over the side and under the counter. As *Tzu Hang*'s stern lifted, I saw quite clearly that the whole of the rudder had gone.

'Don't look now, but the rudder's gone,' I said, when I was down below again.

'What, clean gone?'

'Clean as a whistle. It must have broken off right under the hull.'

'Well,' said Beryl, 'she sails with no one at the helm, so I don't see why she shouldn't sail just as well without it.'

'We'll have to fix a steering-oar,' John said. The matter of a mere rudder, after all that *Tzu Hang* had been through, and in view of all that we had to do, seemed very small.

THE FIRST JURY-RIG

John started work on the new mast that afternoon, while Beryl and I went on with the interminable job of clearing up. We had salvaged only two halves of broken spars from the deck. Half a spinnaker pole, which had remained snapped on to the life-line, where it was stowed, and half a spare staysail boom, which had been lashed down to the deck alongside the dinghies. John started to cut these so that they could be scarfed together. By Monday the mast was finished. It was 15 feet long, scarfed together in a perfect join, riveted through with four copper rivets, and whipped with seizing-wire. On one end was the staysail boom-fitting, to which we could fasten the shrouds and the stays, and on the other was the spinnaker boom snap-hook. We used a spare forestay as the backstay, a spare mizzen-shroud as a forestay, and a jib bridle as the shrouds, which could be adjusted by tackles to the deck.

In order to set up the mast, we fastened the snap-hook to a deck-ring at the foot of the old mainmast position, with the mast lying aft along the deck. Then we fastened the backstay, the forestay, and the shrouds to the mast-head, making all the lower ends secure at approximately their right length, except the forestay. It seems a very simple thing now, putting up a 15-foot mast, but in the conditions that we were working under it was difficult enough. John took the end of the mast, and standing with his legs wide apart and his knees bent, he raised it until I could hold it on the forestay. We pushed and pulled and directly it was upright, although still rather wobbly, John set up the shrouds with the tackles, and I set up the forestay with a rigging-screw fastened to a grommet round the broken bowsprit. We had a mast again. Now we made fast the sheets of the raffee, a small square sail, 2 feet at the top and 10 feet at the foot, and hoisted it.

There was a strong wind blowing, and it plunged and struggled as we hoisted, like a wild horse roped, as if to escape from its task. We subdued it and the moment it was up I felt *Tzu Hang* steady and begin to sail with the wind on her quarter.

'She's sailing, she's sailing!' I shouted in excitement.

But John said, 'Look at the bloody mast!' and I saw that it was bending like a bow. We let the halliard fly, and the sail swooped and cracked, the sheets whipping madly. It had a small 2-foot spar at the head, which used to drive at us when we were setting it up or taking it down, and after one or two vicious assaults we began to regard it with great respect.

'I'll have to strengthen the mast,' John said. And we took the whole thing down again.

On the whole it had been a good day. In the morning, amongst other things, we had actually got the bilges dry, and I had taken the distributor and timing of the motor to pieces and put it in oil, and pumped all the salt water out of the engine sump, and poured oil in the cylinders. John had taken his movie camera to pieces and put it in oil, and Beryl and I wondered how on earth he thought that he could ever assemble it again. We had been sailing for a short time, long enough at any rate to hold out a promise of being able to sail in the near future, and we had found the spare barometer in a locker, in a wet leather case, but otherwise all right. It was reading very low, 28·95. The ship's barometer and the ship's clock had both vanished with the doghouse.

The barometer was reading low for a very good reason. We were in for another gale, and we couldn't have carried any sail anyway. All through the night it blew, with high breaking seas, giving poor Beryl no rest at all. It was obvious that her shoulder was quite badly injured, though whether it was a cracked shoulder bone, or badly torn muscles, I could not say. She managed by day, but at night she could find no comfort, and all we could do for her was to wedge her with cushions, so that she wasn't rolled about. She managed to get some rest with the help of sleeping pills, which we had in the medicine chest.

The wind began to ease before lunch on Tuesday, and I was able to get good sights, although it was quite impossible to stand on the deck to do so. We were in Long. 97° 15′ W. and Lat. 51° 20′ S. Getting a sight was not easy. I stood in the forehatch, with only my head and shoulders out, and took a long series which we averaged out, scrapping any that were obviously wrong. We plotted our position on the *National Geographic* map, but the bottom of the map was filled with insets of the Pacific Islands, so we found we were fifteen miles west of Nuka Hiva.

All over the ship below deck there were small pieces of coke. We found them in drawers, in bookshelves, in our sleeping-bags, and there was almost no place that they hadn't invaded. They had travelled farther and been far more adventurous than the eggs, whose remnants we also found all over the ship. But the eggs had remained on the lower levels. There was even coke on deck, which had been baled out and had stuck in the escape vents. Some of this coke had found its way into the cockpit and into the cockpit drains, and now they were blocked. Looking aft through the window, where we had been wont to see the helmsman's legs, we now saw something like an electric washing machine, one of those with a window in the front, through which you see swirling water. While John set to work to strengthen the mast, I baled out the cockpit, and endeavoured to clear the drains with an ineffectual piece of bent wire.

In the evening the wind was down enough for us to set up the mast again. *Tzu Hang* was on the starboard tack, that is to say she was slowly rolling her way, for she always has some forward movement, down towards the Horn. This time we set the little jib-topsail instead of the raffee, and then we took the dinghy oars, which had been stowed in the stern, and tried to row her round on to the other tack. From the height of *Tzu Hang*'s freeboard, the dinghy oars, which had been stowed in the counter, were hopelessly ineffectual, but we had nothing else. John rowed one way in the bow and I rowed the other way in the stern, and sometimes John came to the stem and rowed with me, but we had no success, and in the end we took the sail down and decided to try again after tea.

When we tried again we set the raffee, and I worked the sheets while John struggled with an oar. There was a big following sea, and gradually we got her stern on to it. For a moment it looked as if it was anyone's bet which way she'd go, but she went on round, and there we were on the port tack, heading north-east. We were sailing. I made a note in the log that night to say that it was our intention to make the rig all secure, to make a steering-oar, and if possible, to build another mast, and to stand on the port tack for Valdivia, Talcahuano, or Valparaiso. That there was beginning to be a change in our feelings is obvious from the log. Bets are recorded for ten shillings on the number of days to land. Beryl said a hundred, John fifty, and I, the lowest and as it turned out the most accurate, said forty. Even Beryl's bet might be described as cautiously optimistic.

But in spite of the optimism, our troubles were by no means over. It blew very hard again, *Tzu Hang* staggered and reeled in the darkness, and even her little bit of rigging blew a thin pipe into the night. In spite of the strengthening to the mast and the middle shrouds that we had put up in addition to the upper shrouds, we began to think that we might lose it, so we were forced to hand the sail. We set it again after breakfast, and I spent another futile morning trying to clear the cockpit drains. Although the cockpit had never seemed to take much water in when the drains were working, it was surprising how quickly it filled, now that they were plugged. Perhaps it was some indication of the type of weather that we were having, because *Tzu Hang* was riding lighter than ever before. Meanwhile John was beginning to dismantle a hanging cupboard to get material for the new mast, and Beryl was busy all day, sorting out tins and making a list of the numbers that were stamped on the lids. All the tins that had been bought were stamped, so that it was possible to identify them from their numbers. For instance, beans were stamped HB 2389 and orange juice OR 4386, or something like that. Our own tins, canned on the farm, we identified roughly from their shape, but there was no knowing whether they would be beef or mutton.

While I was struggling with the cockpit, the sail suddenly began to flutter violently and *Tzu Hang* wore round on to the wrong tack. For the rest of the afternoon, John and I struggled with oars and sheets, in cold squalls of rain and hail, to try and get her back again. The raffee swooped at us, the sheets caught us, like a blow with a cane, across the face; it was still blowing half a gale and there was no hope of doing anything with the big sea that was running, but I was obstinate. Feelings began to rise and we each felt that the other was to blame every time that *Tzu Hang* fell away on to the wrong tack. As we slithered about on our seats, we both tore our oilskin trousers on a broken screw, where the staysail horse had been pulled away. Although we had been wet through for six days now, this tear in the seats of our trousers seemed absurdly important, the crowning hardship of a very poor day. Beryl began to sense tension on deck and put her head out of the hatch. It was the first time that she had appeared, and it was a sign that she was beginning to feel better.

'Come on now, you two,' she said. 'It's tea-time, and don't you think that it would be much better if you stopped struggling and made a steering-oar. Do just leave it now. Leave everything until tomorrow.'

How right she was! We had been living under very strange conditions for a week, with very little sleep, and as far as I was concerned, a lot of anxiety. After all, a day or two wouldn't make much difference. We went below, and Beryl had some special treat for us for tea. Burnt toast, I suppose. The cat was beginning to look dry and wanted to play. We shed off our troubles for the time being, and I think from then on we began to enjoy the trip again. There was, of course, Clio at the back of our minds always, but we had given her a very wide margin for the time when she might expect to hear from us. 'I wonder what on earth she'd think if she could see us now.'

'I think she'd be thrilled to bits,' said John.

'Just think of all the treasures she'd have found in the bilge,' said Beryl.

It was Thursday, February 21, and the wind was dropping. John spent the day making the steering-oar from the corner posts of the doorways leading into the main- and forecabin. Before he started work, he clamped his saw on to a board, and in the dark, heaving cabin, he began to sharpen his saw. It made me think what a bad workman I was, who so rarely sharpened anything, even in the best conditions. After sharpening his saw, he cut scarves and joined them all together to make a 16-foot length, and when the shaft was finished he fastened a locker door on the end to act as a blade.

In the evening we sat by the smoky fire and mended the torn seats of our oilskins with old material and rubber solution.

Our breakfast on that morning had consisted of beans and a boiled egg, three of the twenty-three that we had recovered unbroken, and lunch of soup, biscuits, and jam. For dinner we had a hot beef stew and tinned loganberries. We had drunk for breakfast and tea, a large mug of tea, and at elevenses a tin of orange juice between the three of us. We weren't doing too badly, and that was how we celebrated the end of the first week after the crash.

Next morning John and I went on deck to try out the steering-oar. There was a different feel to the sea, and it looked as if we were in for a pleasanter day. After we had put the sail up, I told John to handle the oar. He had made it, and I wasn't going to risk breaking it. We were still on the starboard tack. He went aft and lashed the oar with a loose lashing to the after chainplate on the port quarter. Then he slipped the oar through the lashing, which he was going to use as a rowlock, until he could bring the blade into the sea. Standing straddled behind the cockpit, his back against the mizzen gallows, the early sun on his fair and now rather long hair, he looked like Eric the Red, conning his Viking ship, and they had other things in common too.

Slowly *Tzu Hang* brought the wind behind her, and slowly, without faltering, she swung on to the other tack. John brought the oar inboard, lashed it to the deck, and came forward looking very pleased with himself.

'Good show, John,' I said. 'It really worked well. That's your oar and I'm damned if I'm going to use it. I might break it.'

'No, I don't think you would,' he said. 'You just have to watch it. It bends a bit. I wish that I'd put a stainless steel wire down the centre so that we wouldn't lose the end if we did. We haven't got that much spare wood.'

As we went below and aft to breakfast, I looked at the small tell-tale compass in the saloon, the only compass that we had now. We were heading west. The wind had backed to the south-east during the night and we had never noticed it. I went forward again and let the sail down. Later, when we came on deck, the sun was shining warmly, the wind had dropped, and the glass was well up. We decided to do no more sailing for that day and to work on the deck. Beryl was able to come up for the first time; the sun and the change gave her a great lift.

The two skylight covers were taken off and the skylights caulked and recovered. Beryl painted them blue, and from then on we were really watertight again. We could not get the ship dry inside as there was so much condensation and so many soaking clothes and cushions, but on this first real chance, the whole deck was littered with clothes, blankets and mattresses.

In the evening we set the raffee again and *Tzu Hang* was sailing along on the right course, once more as if she knew the way. We were off at last. We were in much better condition and even Pwe ventured up during the day. She was horrified at the change in the ship, and, like our cows in Canada when we ploughed up a grass field, she voiced her indignant disapproval; but she stayed on deck while the sun shone.

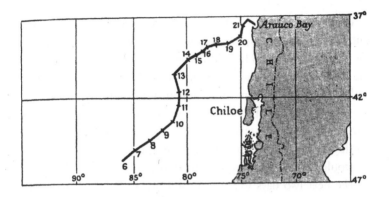

CHAPTER NINE

THE TREK NORTH

WHILE *Tzu Hang* sailed away by herself that evening, she seemed gallant and debonair once more, in spite of her tattered appearance. We started to plan the new rig.

John thought that he could make a square, 20-foot hollow mast, using some floorboards and bunkboards, the ceiling, or inner planking, of the main cabin, and the wood from the hanging cupboard that he was dismantling. He set about drawing a plan. As the boards were only about 5 feet long, there would have to be several butts on each side of the mast. For greater strength these butts would have to be staggered, and opposite each butt there had to be a solid centre to screw them down to. We needed some wood for all these solid centres and also for a spar for the sail. We decided to use the bottom of the old mainmast, which still stood below the deck in the forecabin, 7 feet of solid wood, 6 by 8 inches.

For a new sail we could use the almost unused terylene main-sail, which had been stowed below. If we divided it by unpicking the seam, the bottom half could be used as a lug-sail, and when the time came to re-rig *Tzu Hang*, we could put it together again without doing it any permanent damage. With a 19-foot hoist we would have about 280 square feet of sail, and the mast would have to be properly stayed to stand up to it. Before John started on this he put another perspex light in the other skylight, so that he would have enough light to work below.

The next two days were sunny and dry, with a cold fresh wind blowing, and we were as busy as beavers. We took out the mainmast stump, and I patched the hole in the deck, while John started to saw it up into four lengths. How he did it I don't know. I find ripping a desperate job at the best of times, but he sawed three longitudinal cuts, and then divided each of the four planks, so that he must have sawed 49 feet of wood, in that dark and heaving cabin. As usual the cuts came out straight and true. John would not have dreamed of letting me have a go to help him, and I should have made a mess of it if I had, but it made me tired to watch him. Beryl was up on deck again and at last succeeded, with the dogged pertinacity that makes her such an incalculable force to deal with, in clearing the cockpit drains. That evening she started drying some packets of drinking chocolate on the stove top. We had to taste a spoonful, and it was so good that we ate the whole packet, dipping into it in turn. We turned the night into a bonzo party by drinking a tin of grapefruit juice to finish up with.

While we feasted, we tried to put our impressions together and to find out what had happened to *Tzu Hang*.

John said, 'I think that we were swept by a big wave, and that then we broached to and were rolled over to port, because I know that I was thrown forward and to port first of all. I don't know what happened after that, except struggling under water.'

'I'm certain we didn't broach to, and I'm certain we weren't pooped,' said Beryl. 'I think that I was thrown out, not washed out. I can remember the tremendous steep wave behind us, and I can remember pitching forward out of the cockpit, sort of falling head first, and then being in the water without knowing how I got there.'

'But if we broached to,' I said to John, 'and we swung to starboard, and tripped over our keel, and were rolled over to port, which you are suggesting, how in hell was your tool-box thrown forward, after bursting its lashings, so that it smashed that starboard doorpost there, and landed in the sink?'

'No, that's what beats me absolutely; that's why I don't really think that we broached. But what on earth else could we have done? If we had rolled over after we broached it would account for those marks on the deckhead, and the wet ashes, and all those lockers and drawers being emptied.'

'All the broken masts and spars were to leeward, weren't they?'

'Yes, but I suppose that's another argument in favour of having broached.'

'I don't know. Don't you think that we would have rolled over them, in which case they would all be to weather; and if we had rolled over and not passed over our spars, the shrouds would have been leading underneath the keel, and not across the deck as they were doing. And if we didn't get rolled over how did that tool-box get into the sink.'

'I think that we turned a somersault,' said Beryl.

'If we did turn a somersault, we would be rolling as we came up, and the masts would be canted over one way or the other as we hit the water, and the keel would right her again, rolling her away from her masts. In a matter of a second or two she'd be up and facing the opposite way. Then she'd swing off and there's at least a fifty-fifty chance that her masts would lie to leeward.'

115

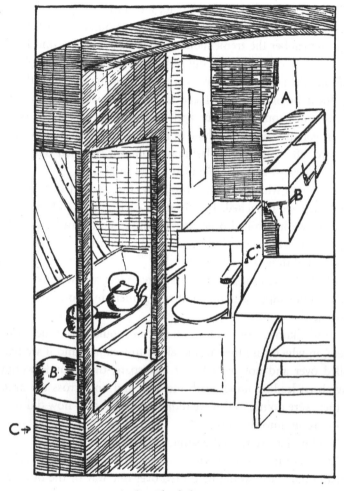

A: Smashed doorpost
B: Tool-box lashed to lockers
B: Tool-box stuck here after breaking loose
C: Water level after smash

RUNNING AND TOWING A HAWSER

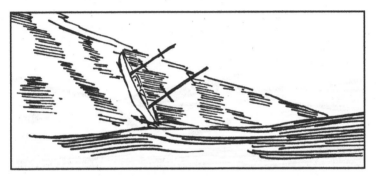

THE BOW GOES IN

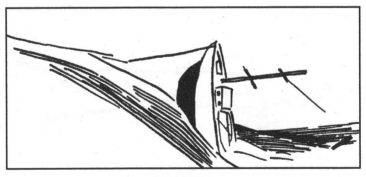

TRIPPING

OVER: FALLING ON TO BEAM ENDS

ROLLING AWAY AND FACING OPPOSITE WAY

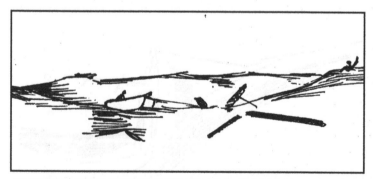

FALLING AWAY BROADSIDE TO SEA, SPARS TO LEEWARD

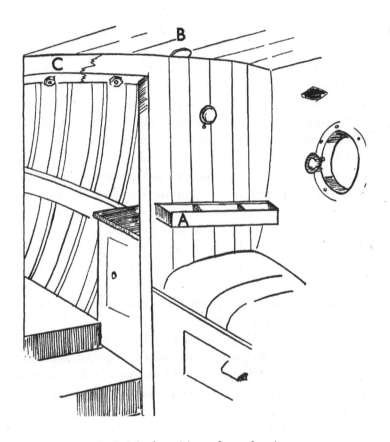

A: Original position of powder-tin
B: Powder-tin caught between bulkhead and deck
C: Broken deck-beam

'That's an idea,' said John. 'If she did do that, as she righted she'd be rolling up, half submerged I suppose, and probably the same wave which turned her up would still be breaking over her, and that's the only way the ports could have been smashed back into the galley and my cabin.'

'I don't know. It's the darnedest thing, but I'm too addled with smoke to think clearly, and I'm really beginning to believe that a somersault is the only reasonable explanation.'

We argued it out on many evenings, but we didn't discover the proof of the somersault theory until weeks afterwards.

The fine weather didn't last long, and for two days we were stopped with a north-east wind, wet mizzling weather, and a falling glass. John had finished sawing up the stump of the mainmast and now the pieces to make the spar were glued and clamped together, and we had to keep the stove going full blast in order to get sufficient heat for the glue to set. While the glue was setting, John was working on the new mast, Beryl on the sail, and I was splicing up the new shrouds. The main cabin was the carpenter's shop, and the spar projected into the forecabin, dividing it into a sailmaker's and a rigger's loft.

I had made an L-shaped chimney out of food tins with their tops cut off and joined together with adhesive tape. The short arm of the 'L' fitted over the fitting for the stovepipe on deck, and the long arm was pointed away from the wind. It was extended as we ate our way through the tins. Later, when it grew longer, it was quite efficient, but at this time it was smoking almost as badly as if we had no chimney at all. Eventually it became so unbearable that I went on deck to alter it. No smoke was coming out of the chimney, but the ventilator, right in the stern, was smoking gaily. I fiddled about with the chimney until a puff of smoke came out again.

'How's that?' I called, cheerful in the clear air. There was a muffled sound of coughing below, and when I got down again, I found the other two with streaming eyes, complaining that it was worse than before. When all work was finished in the evening, we let the stove go out, and found that the chimney in the bathroom had become detached from the deckhead fitting, and the stove was smoking directly into the ship. The stove never stopped smoking, but it improved, and by the time we had no longer the need of a fire, the chimney projected beyond the side of the ship and the smoke problem was nearly solved.

By the 27th the north-east wind had swung round to the north-west and we were able to make sail again. This time we set a mainsail as well as the jib. When *Tzu Hang* had broken away from her masts on the day of the crash, John had transferred the hawser from the stern to the bow, and before coming down to bale, he had attached the working jib to the end, hoping that it might help to hold her bow up to the wind, or at least make a slick to weather. It had had no effect, but the jib had been torn in two up to the bronze luff-rope by the waves. When we brought it in next day we cut the luff-rope and used the upper half to patch the skylights, and now used the lower half as a mainsail, setting it upside down. The sun was struggling fitfully through the cloud layer and the glass was falling. By four o'clock in the morning, it was blowing a gale again, and we took down the little mainsail which had been doing great work pressed flat against the shrouds. We set the raffee and, though it was so small, it towed us strongly to the north. By midday we were into the forties. The mast was going well, and we put a stainless steel radio aerial into the centre.

John was working all day with the mast, fitting his boards together, drilling and countersinking his screw holes, and screwing it all up. He was quite oblivious of his surroundings, oblivious of the weather outside, and of the motion within. With the materials at his disposal he was doing the best that could be done. Time meant nothing to him, perfection everything.

'There is a river, a river of no return,' he sang mournfully as he worked. It was the end of the third week after the crash, and Beryl celebrated it by brushing her hair and washing her face.

'Good heavens, look, who have we got here?' John asked when she came back into the main cabin.

'Little sunshine,' I said. 'Thank goodness she's washed her face.' I looked at the wound on the top of her head and saw that it had healed in a thin white line.

'I thought that it was much worse, and I didn't want it fiddled with, or I'd have washed it sooner. It's probably been healed for days.'

'What about giving us a treat now, and changing out of the McLeod tartan.'

'No, I'm not changing until we make our landfall.' She was quite firm about that, but she gave us fudge for our weekly celebration, and there were treats on the next day too, in celebration of Clio's birthday.

On this day the wind strengthened continuously with dark squalls sweeping up from the south-west, and *Tzu Hang* fled to the north. In the evening for a time she was doing four knots, with the big swells all wrinkled with squalls, and white crests everywhere, leaving their fading tracks across the sea. There was light, and colour and shade, and it was impossible to believe *Tzu Hang* was the wreck that she was. By noon next day we had done sixty miles on the log and seventy-two by observation, and we were in a north-going current. She relished the sea and the day, and she had a quick corkscrew motion, as if she wanted to buck us off the deck in her good spirits. 'I'm the same ship, the same ship,' she seemed to say to us, 'and I know the way. I'll take you to port.' After a particularly bad squall in the evening, which fell upon us with a hissing rush of almost horizontal rain, we took the mainsail down. During the night the raffee kept flopping aback and banging its sheets on the deck, but each time *Tzu Hang* came back to her course without our interference.

All the week the work went on below. The sailmaker stitched away at her tabling and her grommets, and the rigger twisted and poked, and pricked himself, and cursed as amateur riggers and exsoldiers do. John had set us such a high standard of craftsmanship that everything had to be ship-shape and Bristol fashion. The mast was finished on March 4, and John spent a happy day putting in a sheave on a stainless steel pinion in the mast-head, lining the slot in the mast-head with copper sheeting, and putting a wind indicator at the truck on a mahogany cap, and fitting tangs of copper sheeting, bolted through the mast, for the shrouds. He must have felt very proud of it. I do not remember the exact measurements now, but it was approximately 4 by 4 inches at the base, 20 feet long, and tapered to the top. The planks at the sides were ¾ inch, and fore and aft ½ inch. He oiled it with linseed oil, but before we could take it out on deck we had to dismantle it to get it through the hatch.

'How awful,' I said, 'I hate undoing anything once it's done up.'

'Nothing to it, man,' he said. 'You just undo a few screws and it comes apart.' He undid them but the mast didn't come apart.

'Must've missed a screw,' he said, turning the mast round. 'Now, you give a pull, will you?' But the mast still refused to come apart.

Beryl was watching, and after a time she said, 'Isn't there a radio aerial or something holding it together?'

Of course there was, and John had to take off a piece of one side of the mast and cut it.

We put the mast together again on the deck and lashed it down. John went back to gluing the last piece on the spar, so that he had a 12-foot spar. On the next day he shaped it, tapering it at both ends, and put brass sheeting round the centre, so that we could attach the shackle of the halliard. The whole cabin floor was covered with heaps of shavings, which we stuffed into tins to use in lighting the fire. Everything was finished by the end of the fourth week, and we set up the mast.

In order to set up the mast we took the mainsail down, and we used the main halliard to hoist it into position immediately behind the little mainmast that was in use. Otherwise we used the same procedure as before, and with Beryl to help now, everything went smoothly. The mast was stepped on a special step that we had cut out and screwed on to the deck. After it was all set up we took down the original jury-main, stowed it on deck for the time being, and then we adjusted the rigging-screws and set all sail. The mast looked a much better job than the old one, with its neatly finished shrouds and stays, and it gave us more sail. The mainsail set higher, and we could now set the storm-jib upside down as a jib. The new mainsail was ready by the evening and we looked forward to trying it out with some excitement. That evening, when we switched on the radio, the voice of the B.B.C. came clearly over the air. 'The talk tonight,' said a smooth and cultured voice, and we imagined the spotted tie and the neatly folded handkerchief, 'is on modern travel. The emphasis today is on speed, comfort, and security.'

We had our new mast, but we had done wonderfully well on the old one. Since we first set it up we had made good 750 miles, and during the last two days we had made runs on the log of 70 and 75 miles, and 188 miles in the two days by observation. It looked as if we were still getting a good lift from the current.

When we put the new sail up next morning it looked enormous, and the moment *Tzu Hang* felt it, she stopped her cavorting, and steadied down to real sailing, her wake rippling away behind her, but the centre of effort was too far forward, and she began to pay off slowly, coming before the wind. We took a reef in the sail on account of the freshening wind, and hauled the tack down to the foot of the mast. With the storm-jib set she balanced nicely with the wind on her quarter, and when we hauled the sheet in, she brought the wind almost abeam.

That was an improvement, because before she would only sail with the wind on the quarter, but to be sure of getting in to port, she had to go to windward. It was no good sitting back and hoping that a fair wind would blow us there. In order to try her to windward we set up the old foremast as a mizzen with the same rigging that it had had before, and using the old jib that had brought us so far as a sail, with a plank tacked on to it as a boom. As soon as it was up and hauled as close as we could make it, *Tzu Hang* began to swing to windward. I felt a surge of relief, thinking now that nothing should stop us.

'She's going to windward, she's going to windward,' I shouted, exulting, to Beryl.

John was bent down low by the mast. He held the mast with both hands, and he looked anxiously up its length to the truck, so that if the mast had not been there, he would have been in an attitude of supplication, like a knight asking for strength for his sword.

'Here, come quickly,' he called to me, but it was too late, and as I reached him, there was a crack and the noise of splintering wood. The mast broke in two above the middle shrouds and fell into the sea.

We pulled it back again, and Beryl and I were distressed, not because of the mast being broken, but because of John and all the hours of work that he had put into it in that dark and smoke-filled cabin.

'Poor John,' she said, but he was quite unperturbed.

'Never mind,' he said, 'we'll fix her up tomorrow.'

We lay for the rest of that day and night, and all the following morning, while John worked on the mast. It wasn't worth moving the mizzen forward again, and anyway it was blowing hard once more; a last flick of those westerly winds which had chased us so far across the ocean, and nearly under the sea. But it was a friendly sort of flick, a kind of 'Off you go, and don't come back again when I'm busy.'

It was not a difficult repair job, and the mast was two inches shorter when it was finished. John strengthened it by screwing extra planks into the sides, but we decided that we would not use the big sail except in a light wind.

'I've really enjoyed making it,' he said, when it was ready again, 'it's been a good sort of feeling, knowing that so much depended on my skill. A hell of a lot of good a college education is in a situation like this. I don't think I'm going to worry about missing that any more.'

We had had a rough and uncomfortable night, and it was rough enough to give us a difficult task in setting the mast up. This time we had no mast to raise it with, but we took the forestay to the winch, and winched it up while John raised it, and Beryl held the foot against the step. There were some exciting moments until the backstay tightened, and the shrouds were set up. As soon as the mast was in position, we set the torn jib on the main, and were off again; a great relief to be sailing, after being stopped for twenty-four hours. We celebrated with plum pudding.

THE FINAL JURY-RIG

On March 10 we were running well with the raffee and the main. Beryl was patching the little storm-jib to make a mizzen sail, and John was making a gooseneck to fit an oar, so that it could be used as a boom for the mizzen. In the afternoon the wind strengthened and came more from the north-west, so that *Tzu Hang* began to fall off in her course. We set the mizzen and she came back again. Then she began to point a little high, so we reefed it, this tiny little sail; it made just the required difference, and she held to her course once more. For the next two days we made great running, but the wind was hauling round to the south, and we found ourselves sailing west of north, away from the coast of Chile, so we went to the starboard tack. We decided to make Mocha Island our landfall; Mocha Island which Drake had visited on his way up from Magellan and had gained some information about the Spaniards on the mainland. We were into the south winds now, the south winds and the northerly drift of the Humboldt current, and we would have to watch the current, so that we were not carried north of the port that we were aiming for.

The setting up of this mast marked a new phase in our journey since the smash. The first phase had been the struggle for survival, the second one of hope and hard work, and now, and until we closed the Chilean coast, we could imagine almost that we were cruising again. We were much more relaxed and had no serious work to do. It was warmer, and we spent much of our time on deck. Most of the books had been tightly jammed in their shelves, so there was still something to read. The fishing rod was brought out, and John amused himself by making lures from fish-hooks and wool of various colours. He preferred to catch a fish on something that he had made himself, rather than on one of the spoons that we still had on the ship. He spent hours also in re-assembling his camera. When everything was fitted together again, he found that he had a small spacing washer left over. But on the second attempt he succeeded in making it run again. In the evening we used to play a home-made game of scrabble.

We decided to make for Talcahuano, the Chilean Navy Base, for I knew that they had many links with the British Navy and that they would probably be able to give us some assistance. Beryl had been in Chile two years before the war, when she had done a great ride up the Western Cordillera from Magallanes. She had stayed in Talcahuano with a friend, whose name she remembered. The house was on a cliff over the sea, and there was a white rock in the water beneath it, but she had heard that the house had been destroyed in the earthquake.

'Directly I get in,' I said, 'I'm going to get hold of the Consul and get him to take me round to the Admiral. I'm sure that we'll never be able to get her repaired unless we can get a hand from the Navy.'

'When you get hold of the Admiral, you might ask him if he's got a daughter,' John said. 'I'd like to meet her.'

'What's all this?' said Beryl. 'It's much too early to start talking like that, certainly about daughters. He'll probably have a dozen, all strictly chaperoned. We made this mistake, talking too much, before. You must not say "when," only "if." The Chilean girls were lovely though.'

'I think that it is very much an "if" as far as Talcahuano is concerned,' I said, 'because if the south wind blows as it's supposed to, all the time in summer, it will be blowing right out of the bay and it has a very narrow entrance. I don't think that we'd be able to beat it in this rig.'

'You might do it on the tide,' John said.

'But the trouble is this current setting up the coast. We can't hang about waiting for the tide because we'd be carried past, and if we were past an entrance we'd never get back against the wind and the current. We've got to do it first shot.'

'If you don't make it and there are lovely Chilean girls waiting, I'm going to swim for it!'

'Anyway, there won't be any quarantine for cats, will there, Pwe?' Pwe was looking much better.

'If a ship came along and offered us a tow now, would you take it?' John asked.

'What, after coming all this way by ourselves …?'

But Beryl answered before I could. She said 'No' firmly.

There seemed to be a better alternative than Talcahuano. Ten miles south of it was Arauco Bay. Once inside Arauco Bay we would be in comparatively sheltered waters. It had two entrances, one on each side of Santa Maria Island, and the northern one was wide and easy to get into. Within the bay were the ports of Coronel and Lota, and if we couldn't make them we could still find an anchorage in shallow water, protected from the south and south-west wind.

The beginning of the fifth week brought a different feel to the ship. We were getting near to land. Three hundred miles seemed nothing after such a long journey, and I was continually looking to the east, hoping to see the Cordillera against the sky, and knowing at the same time that I couldn't. There were low solid clouds far beyond the horizon, stretching up and down the Chilean coast. With the warmer weather Beryl and John decided to have a wash. I was more energetic and bathed, putting on goggles, and diving down to look at the rudder fittings. The broken rudder-post projected just below the hull, and the fittings on the stern-post were all intact. The water was very cold and I nipped back quickly.

We began to see porpoises again, and supposed that it was a sign of more fish on the continental shelf, for we had seen very few on our way over. Floating patches of seaweed and seabirds with a shorter cruising range than the albatrosses, the petrels and the shearwaters, put in their appearance, and on the 16th I saw a bird flying north with a small landbird's dipping flight. I did not recognise him then, but next morning there were any number about. They were gay little phalaropes, spinning round and round in the water, and hopping about in and on the patches of seaweed.

The colours also were lovely. In the evening the upper sky was covered with lacy filaments of wind-blown cloud, rose pink in the setting sun, and the whole evening sky was lightly painted in a variety of pastel shades darkening down into the dusk of the eastern horizon, with a white cloud showing low across it, which our imagination could turn easily into the snow peaks of the Andes. Night after night now we had this display of colour, so different from the dark, low, driven clouds of further south. As the colours faded, the moon showed with Jupiter bright and almost in her arms. It was like coming down to a base camp from a high mountain, with water running and some gentians showing in the grass.

Now that we were in the southerly winds and out of the boisterous westerlies, our progress was slower. On March 19, a great
skua was round again, with his quick determined wing-beat. A
bird of ill-omen, I thought, but he brought some luck, because
John caught an albacore on his home-made lure. There was great
excitement when it was brought on board and dropped flapping in
the cockpit. Pwe was delighted at the prospect of fish for dinner,
and walked round purring and rubbing against our legs, until I
gave her a fishtail to keep her quiet. On a fish diet she started to
swell visibly.

Next morning Beryl was up early when she called down to us
from the deck that she could see land. There was cloud all over,
low overcast, and after some time I picked out a dim vertical line,
showing hazily behind some rain on the horizon to the south. A
landfall after so long a journey, and so many hazards, is something to be remembered, but John stayed in his bunk below, and
I believe that for a moment he was really quite sorry that the trip
was coming to an end. While I had been restless because of our
slow advance during the past few days, both he and Beryl had
been quite happy, enjoying the rest and the warmer weather, and
knowing that in a few days, if we made our port, we would be
wrapped up in all kinds of problems again. John, like the cat, had
begun to put on weight.

The vertical line was a cliff, the north-east edge of Mocha
Island, but it soon vanished in some cloud, and it was impossible
to say how far away we were from it. I guessed about twenty to
thirty miles. We laid a course now by compass, the little tell-tale
compass which we had in the main cabin, for Tulcapel Point. It
was not adjusted for the southern hemisphere, and always tried
to point through the earth to the north pole, so that it had to be
tilted to get a reading, but like so many other things on the boat,

it served. The whole of the land seemed to be wrapped in fog. I could make nothing of it, and gradually the fog closed around us, so that it was impossible to get a proper fix. For a moment I saw the outline of a cape ahead of us, but before it could be identified it was gone again.

A shark followed us lazily, keeping station ten yards astern, although locally they are not supposed to come so far south, and eight little petrels in a gossip upon the water raised their wings and danced away on their feet from the slowly questing bow. We passed many patches of weed with their busy little travellers, the phalaropes, skipping about upon them. Towards evening I began to be anxious and to think that we were south of Tulcapel Point, and getting to the wide, shallow, and open bay south of that headland, where the Pilot warned that the sea might break two miles out to sea. But just before dark we saw, close to, a sandy shelving beach with the dark outline of a headland behind, looking as if it was separated from a round mushroom island by a narrow channel. Tulcapel and Morguilla Island perhaps, the best bet anyway, so we put *Tzu Hang* round on the steering-oar, and out on the starboard tack. The fog still hung round us after supper, but there was a faint light in the sky to starboard, filtering through the murk, which might have been the lights of the coal-mine at Tulcapel, and below it for a moment one light appeared and disappeared. We held away on the port tack and thick fog wrapped us round.

In the morning the sea around us was clear again, but between us and the shore lay a white curtain, so that we might have been sixty miles away at sea. I was able to get a position line, but before I could get a fix, a dark low cloud came rolling up from the south, gathering the fog curtain in to it, and drawing it round us as it spread over the sky, and once more we were surrounded in a dull greyness, with the sea rolling up out of the murk, and rolling on into it again.

As far as I could make out, when I plotted *Tzu Hang*'s estimated position, we were fifteen miles south-west of Punta Lavapie, the southern entrance to Arauco Bay. When the fog came down we stopped sailing, but I reckoned that we had about twenty miles to sail, if we kept on this course, before we turned to run in. The second leg, to bring us into the bay, should be about eleven miles.

We set sail again on the same course, nearly due north, at four o'clock in the afternoon, with a light breeze from the south-west. At about eleven, when I thought that the mileage we had covered and the current had brought us far enough and that it was nearly time to go on to the other tack, we stopped. We waited until two in the morning, hoping for another mile or so on the current, and not wanting to close the land before daylight.

At two we made sail again, and headed in for the shore. We started in moonlight, but in an hour we were in thick fog again. Daylight came, and we kept a watch at the bow. After eleven miles, when I thought that we should either be in the bay or close on shore, we were still in thick fog. All kinds of seabirds were in the water and went splattering away from the bows of the ship, as she came upon them in the mist, but I could hear no other sound than the sound of the seabirds and the slap of a wave and the noise of *Tzu Hang*: no sound of breakers and no sound of a horn. It took nearly a quarter of a mile to wear the ship round, and I didn't like to think of the difficulties that we might get into if I was wrong.

'It's no good,' I said, 'I'm not going on until after breakfast. We may just as well give it a little longer.'

I could see that both Beryl and John were disappointed, John particularly so, because I am sure that if he had been alone he would have gone ahead, and now that he was so near he wanted to make a job of it and get in that day.

'Sorry, John,' I said, and he was touched because I had understood.

'Hell, you can't go in when you can't see,' he said.

But after breakfast, when I felt braver, we made sail again. There seemed to be a difference in the sea, as if we were getting into the shelter of a headland, and the waves were certainly altering. And then suddenly there was the faint ball of the sun showing through the fog. I went below to have another look at the makeshift chart I had made, and while I was still below, I heard Beryl call that the fog was clearing, and before I got up to see I heard her shout, 'Land, I see land.' Even John found this exciting. To the south of us and a mile away were some rocky islets, and beyond them were the bold cliffs of Santa Maria Island. We were entering Arauco Bay.

The sea fell calm. The sun shone and the sky came blue above us. Behind us the fog lay like a white wall across the entrance to the bay. Fourteen miles away across the bay, on the other side, we could make out a low coastline and some buildings, which we thought must be Coronel, and tree-clad foothills, blue in haze, climbing up to the cloudridden mountains behind. North of us three hills showed their tops close together above the white line of the fog, the Bio Bio Hills. We sat on deck, all anxiety gone, while the rudderless ship sailed herself quietly to her port across the bay.

Slag-heaps we saw now, and the buildings began to find individuality from the jumble that we had seen in the distance. As we closed the shore we began to see tawdry lines of shacks, miners' cottages we supposed, on sunbaked grassless earth, and stacks of coal, and a long loading wharf below. Beyond it was a wooden wharf, and we sailed in the evening slowly towards it. From the wooden wharf a low shore ran round to an untidy little town and the whole was topped by a vast cemetery, the most striking landmark from the sea.

Near the wharf and on the shore there was a row of huts with yellow fish-boats drawn up on the beach. As we drew near there was a rush to launch them and the fishermen and boys rowed out around us, laughing and chattering in Spanish. They showed us where to anchor and they gripped the bulwark with their hands. Their boats bumped against *Tzu Hang*'s sides and they swarmed on board at any unprotected point. Beryl was the only one of us who could speak any Spanish. After a time with many '*Por favor Señor*'s we persuaded them to leave us because we wanted to eat, and they rowed off again to their village.

That night we lay rocking gently at our anchor as we had done at Dromana, nearly three months ago and over 6,000 miles away. I thought before I went to sleep of the path that we had followed and of how *Tzu Hang* had sailed her devious way, with so little help from us. And I thought of Slocum and the Pilot of the *Pinta*. It almost seemed as if *Tzu Hang* had had a Pilot too.

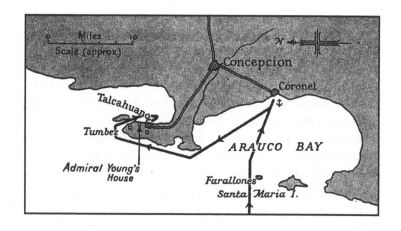

CHAPTER TEN

FIRST DAYS IN CHILE

Tzu Hang lay that night pulling lightly at her chain, easing forward and lying back again, and rolling gently in the moonlight. She seemed at ease and resting, satisfied that for the time being her work was done. I awoke many times to wonder at the stillness and stayed awake to marvel that we were at anchor once again, finding it almost impossible to believe that we were really in port, in a safe harbour. Daylight came, and soon afterwards a chattering outside, like sparrows in the ivy. The chorus grew and closed around us and then there was a ponderous thump against *Tzu Hang*'s side.

I had been lying in a torpor of relaxation, thinking comfortably of going ashore and of visiting a new land, but the thump brought me jumping to my feet. Beryl had given John and me a

136

short lecture on the necessity for the courteous forms of address, no matter what the stress, while we were in South America, and now she hissed a warning to me as I left the cabin. I had a false and twisted smile by the time my head was out of the hatch. There was a crowd of little yellow-painted fish-boats round the ship, and men and boys in ragged clothes, with laughing sunburnt faces. The leader of those who had helped us to the anchorage, and who had told us that his name was Oscar, had his hands on the rail and was grinning across the deck at me; a long knife scar showed livid across his cheek. His heavy boat, its bow shod with a piece of rusty iron, was pounding against *Tzu Hang*, but he was quite unaware that it might do her any damage.

'*Buenos días,*' I said, and at this example of my fluency he skipped nimbly on board, flooding me in a torrent of Spanish. The last thing that we wanted before breakfast was a visit from these laughing, inquisitive, and nimble-fingered fisherfolk, for a quick look round the deck showed that anything loose had already vanished during the night. With Oscar as the advance guard, the other boats began to close in rapidly.

'No *Señor,*' I cried, '*abhi khana khaenge,*' suddenly afflicted with Hindustani. 'Beryl, for God's sake come and talk to these people or we'll have the whole ship full of them.'

Beryl came up on deck and John put his head out of the hatch; we watched her as children watch a conjuror and his hat. '*Buenos días,*' she said, and there was a polite reply from the boats around. '*Por favor, Señores, ahora no queremos más hombres auf dem bâteau. Queremos desayuno, más tarde ustedes.*' She accompanied this multilingual effort with vigorous signs. Oscar's mobile and scar-divided face lit with greeting, went blank at the foreign words, brightened again with understanding, and finally flushed with anger, which he turned on his compatriots in our defence.

They took themselves off to their fishing with some salty remarks at Oscar's expense, and he settled himself on *Tzu Hang*'s deck, talking lazily to his companion in the boat, who fended it off from *Tzu Hang* with a negligent bare foot, and sometimes let it bump against her side.

While we were still eating our breakfast Oscar took himself off in response to a hail from the shore and was soon back again with another agonising bump and a young sailor, smartly turned out in what we came to recognise later as the fatigue dress of the Chilean Navy, blue jeans, and an American sailor's cap. Oscar had established himself and his boat, to his considerable profit, as handyman and tender to *Tzu Hang*. Our new visitor represented, as far as we could make out, the Customs Officer, the Quarantine Officer, and the Harbour Master, all of whom were waiting for me in the offices of the Port Authority in Coronel. I finished my breakfast, collected what remained of the ship's papers, and went ashore.

We tied up at an old wooden wharf on twisted and worn piles, and walked along it avoiding the numerous holes in the decking, and out through some battered gates on to a narrow dusty street. It was warm and bright on shore and a fresh clean wind was already blowing in from the sea, tossing some paper in the gutter, eddying round a warehouse at the end of the wharf, and blowing a wisp of dust across the road. With a loud blare on its horn, a fat white-topped bus came rushing round the corner, and just missed a long-bodied and short-legged dog, which ran out from under a fruit stall at the side of the road. On the top of the bus, above the windscreen, the word *Microbus* was printed, and on the window, 'Coronel—Concepcion'. We found that *Microbus*, or colloquially *Micro* or *Gondola*, was the generic term for all motor buses in Chile, but this one had a personal name also, painted on its broad, blue, and dusty behind. It was called *La Estrellita* or little star. *La*

Estrellita sent a cloud of dust over some great clusters of grapes in the fruit store, and a broad-hipped, red-faced woman leant over the counter and blew the dust away with gusty blasts. As she did so she talked, in between blasts, to a man with a wooden leg and a brown poncho thrown over his shoulder. A wine bottle poked its head out of his pocket.

It was my first impression of Chile, and the country seemed warm and welcoming, as did some of the dark-eyed bold-looking girls I noticed, as we walked up the street of little shops and stores. Oscar followed close behind, explaining to anyone who cared to listen the object of our journey, and giving the latest reports on the new arrival in the bay. As we approached the harbour offices he began to lag behind, and by the time that we entered, he had disappeared.

If there was any reason for him to have avoided the offices, he need have had no fear, for there was no one there. In the main office there was a table and two chairs, and against the wall on a small table, a old typewriter with ivory keys, but none of the officers that I had understood were waiting. In the adjoining room, which was also empty, there was a fine looking radio-telephone apparatus and a large wall clock with no glass, and the minute hand bent out 2 inches from its face. The sailor offered me a cigarette and a chair, said to me '*Un momento*' and went into the radio room, where he started to read a paper that had been tucked underneath the set. I noticed that the clock had stopped.

After twenty minutes a man in civilian clothes came in. He bowed to me and wished me good day, and went in to join the sailor. After a time he went to the radio-telephone and began to turn the dials. '*Alo, alo, alo,*' he called several times without any response, and then switched off the set without any sign of annoyance, and continued his talk with the sailor. After another twenty minutes and another attempt by the radio operator to establish communication, without any apparent result, I thought of John and Beryl, impatient to come ashore, and decided that I would wait no longer for any authority. I made the sailor understand that I must go and speak to the Consul.

'Very well,' he said, 'we will go and see Don Santiago.'

We found Don Santiago sitting in the inner office of an agency representing various firms, and looking after the interests of the Pacific Steam Navigation Company, in one of whose ships he had sailed fifty years before, as assistant purser. As young James Monks, from Liverpool, he had come ashore, and he had stayed on to become Don Santiago, known and respected by everyone in Coronel, with the manners of a Spanish hidalgo, and an ever-growing brood of attractive grandchildren. It turned out that Don Santiago was not the Consul, but an honorary assistant in Coronel, and that the real Consul was in Concepcion. With a vague grasp of our story he rang up Concepcion, and passed on a surprisingly new version of our doings.

The Consul took it all in his stride, and when I was able to prise Don Santiago off the telephone, and speak to him myself, he said that he would get into touch with Admiral Young, a retired officer of the Chilean Navy, and find out how best we could be repaired. He said also that he would be out in the afternoon, and that he'd take us all back to Concepcion, for dinner and a bath.

Over the mantelpiece in Don Santiago's office was the picture of a full-rigged ship, and before I hurried off to give John and Beryl the news, I asked him about it.

'It is the picture of a ship that was wrecked on Santa Maria Island in a fog, while trying to come into Arauco Bay. Many ships were lost that way,' he said. 'I got it from the captain's cabin after she was wrecked. I was a young lad then.' As I left he called to me to tell me not to worry about the Customs, and to say that he would speak to them for me.

On the way back to the ship Oscar joined me suddenly at a corner carrying a bunch of grapes for Beryl. I wondered who had paid for them: and when we passed the harbour offices an unruffled voice was still calling '*Alo, alo, alo.*'

The yellow fish-boats were clustered round *Tzu Hang* like wasps round a jam-pot at afternoon tea in the garden.

'It's no good,' said Beryl, 'we just can't keep them away. We'll have to leave Oscar in charge when we go ashore. Poor *Tzu Hang*. When the boats bump her like this it's like kicking her when she's down. It's driving John crazy too. He's not used to this sort of people.'

John and I went ashore again to get our hair cut. Mine had been trimmed by Beryl just before the smash, but John had a luxuriant growth, and the irrepressible Oscar kept patting himself behind the ears, in an effeminate gesture, and laughing slyly at John. After the losses from the deck and the continuous bumping of the small boats, John was in no mood for such trivialities, and I could see that his temper was rising, but Oscar, the ape, was quite unaware of the tornado that was threatening to engulf him.

After lunch we all three went up to Don Santiago's office leaving Oscar and his mate, like wolves to guard a lamb, in charge of poor *Tzu Hang*. Don Santiago was very doubtful about our choice of a watchman, as well he might be, but we thought that *Tzu Hang* was in such poor condition that no one would think of despoiling her further, and that setting a thief to catch a thief was perhaps the best procedure. In fact, after being so long at sea, we didn't think too ill of anyone: we were suckers on shore.

Leslie Pountney, the kindly and urbane British Consul from Concepcion, was waiting for us with Don Santiago, and we set off in his car on our way to Concepcion, twenty miles away along a straight flat road, through burnt grasslands, and young plantations of New Zealand pine. The old indigenous trees had long ago gone from the surrounding country. On our left the flat pasture ran down to the sea, and on our right the foothills rose in careless disarrangement to the distant central plain, and beyond again, the white tooth of an Andean peak showed above the shoulders of a nearer hill.

There was not much traffic on the road, but what there was was varied. Two small barefooted boys, riding bareback, galloped down the verge. We passed a number of trucks and lorries, one or two microbuses, a couple of oxcarts, and a horseman dressed in a short embroidered poncho, a flat black and wide-brimmed hat, wooden box stirrups, and vast silver spurs. As we neared Concepcion, the road crossed on a long bridge the dry bed of the Bio Bio River, dry now because it was the end of the summer, but in winter a wide brown flood, which took its annual toll of drowned from country ferries and overloaded little boats.

During the drive the Consul told us the impressive story of what he had been doing on our behalf. He had spoken to Admiral Young, who considered that the only possible place to get the yacht repaired was in the Navy Yard at Talcahuano. He had also spoken to Captain Wilson, who was Chief of Staff in Talcahuano, who was coming to see us on the following day to let us know what they would be able to do for us. Meanwhile we would have to arrange a tow round to Talcahuano. The Navy couldn't do this as they would have to send an ocean-going tug at quite prohibitive cost, but the Consul thought that we could arrange this tow with Señor Querello, who owned a fish-meal factory and some ocean-going fish-boats which kept the factory supplied.

We went in search of Señor Querello, who arrived at his house at about the same time as we did. He was just back from his farm

142

in the country, and the back of his truck was loaded with grapes. He was sunburnt, vigorous, and gay, and he swept us all into his house, where a lovely dark girl, his wife, poured out wine for us. After a time the Consul told him our story and we were able to follow the conversation.

'Do you think you could help them?' the Consul asked.

'*¿Cómo no?*'

'Would you be able to send one of your boats round to Coronel to tow them to Talcahuano?'

'*¿Cómo no?*'

Beryl and I looked at each other. It seemed as if the first obstacle was going to be overcome.

'They would like to pay for the tow of course.'

'*Nada, nada,*' said Señor Querello, 'it is nothing. We are people of the sea, and would like to help them.'

I think that there can be no one, who has built or repaired a boat anywhere, who has not been astounded at the cost, frustrated at the delays, and exasperated at all kinds of unforeseen difficulties. We went through it all in the next few months, but the experience was softened by this kind of generosity and undemanding kindness, that we met with everywhere in Chile. As for Señor Querello, I think that we remembered him every day with gratitude, during the rest of our stay in Chile, as the smell of his fish-meal factory wafted across the road to us, on our daily journey from Concepcion to Talcahuano.

Before returning to *Tzu Hang* we revelled in a hot bath and a good dinner at the Consul's comfortable flat, and we sent a twenty-one word cable to Clio telling her as much as we could of the story.

Captain Wilson and his Señora arrived on board next morning. They looked as if they had just stepped out of a fashion-plate, but they both squeezed down through the forehatch and into the damp and musty-smelling cabin. As Señora Wilson looked around her at the mildewed teak, the scarred deckhead blackened with smoke from the fire, the stripped ceiling and the missing doorposts, she exclaimed with charming courtesy, '*¡Qué linda, que preciosa!*' Captain Wilson had been on the staff of the naval attaché in London and spoke English well. He had also commanded the *Esmeralda*, the sail training-ship of the Chilean Navy. The command of the training-ship seemed to be one of the best appointments in the Chilean Navy, and this sail training opened an easy door for us in our relations with the Navy officers, all of whom went through it, and were as a result particularly interested in *Tzu Hang* and her voyage.

'The Admiral says,' Captain Wilson told us now, 'that he will be very glad for your yacht to be repaired in the Navy Yard. Of course there will be charges, but as in Chile we like to encourage sport we will try and keep them down.'

'Will we be able to work on her ourselves?'

'Oh yes, of course. The only thing is that because it is a private yacht, you will have to buy all the materials outside the Arsenale, as it's called. We have to conform with the regulations, you know. But as for assistance, I'm sure that we will be able to give you a lot of assistance, and it's only the specialised labour that we will have to charge you for.'

As soon as Captain Wilson and his trim Señora had left us, I turned to John.

'Well what do you think of it?'

'Sounds all right, sounds pretty good. We'll have to rustle up some wood, and I suppose they'll let us have a place to work in. I wonder what sort of machines they've got.'

'Does that mean you're really going to be able to stay on and help us fix her up?'

'Well I've been thinking. I really could stay on for a month or so, but as you won't be going round the Horn now, I think I'll have to leave you then. I've got to get to South Africa, and then I've got to go back to *Trekka* in New Zealand, but I sure would like to fix her up again for you. I feel I owe it to her. I'll build the doghouse and the skylights and the masts, and you ought to be able to manage the rest.'

'Good man.'

I think Beryl had known all the time that he would stay on, but it was a tremendous relief to me to know that we were going to have his skill and knowledge for the refitting, and as for the Horn. ... I thought that we'd had a good shot, and soon it would be winter. I thought that Beryl and I would take *Tzu Hang* the easier way home, by way of Panama.

Next morning before six o'clock we heard the noise of an engine and the thud of bare feet on the deck. I looked out to find a beamy powerful fish-boat already making fast its towrope, and two stalwart seamen preparing to get up our anchor. The captain of the fish-boat was young and athletic, with a clear-cut aquiline face, and he was wearing a black shirt and a black Spanish hat, so that he looked as if he should be riding in the Feria at Seville, rather than on the deck of a fishboat. He came on board for a time during the tow and we offered him some breakfast, but he refused, saying that he never ate at sea but only drank wine, and sometimes he was at sea for three days.

The morning mist was hanging low about us when we started off, but it soon began to rise and thin, and the sun burst through and shredded it into faint vanishing streamers. Away to port we could see Santa Maria Island and the Farallones, where big ships had been lost, groping their way into Arauco Bay in a fog, but which *Tzu Hang* had providentially avoided. Soon the blue outline of the Bio Bio Hills showed to starboard, and ahead was Punta Gualpen, the southern end of the Tumbez Peninsula, round which we would go to enter Talcahuano. In three hours we were well out of the bay, and into the ocean swell, rolling up the indented coastline of the peninsula.

Beryl pointed to a guano-covered rock in a little bay, with pelicans perched upon it. 'I'm sure that's where I used to bathe,' she said, 'and Tanny's house, where I stayed, was just up on the cliff above. I believe it was destroyed in the earthquake soon after I left.' As we were looking for it the towrope broke. We picked up the end and passed it back to our tug, but it parted again so we passed them one of our lines, and that brought us into smooth water again, in the Boca Chica, a narrow passage between Quinquina Island and the southern shore. I was glad that we hadn't attempted to come in under our jury-rig.

Another mile or so and we were passing down a long stone breakwater, the outer wall of the Arsenale, and then down and under the stem of the Chilean battleship *Latorre* once H.M.S. *Canada*, who fought at Jutland and now was immobile and outdated and shortly to be scrapped, but with her great racecourses of decks, her huge guns and her severe uncluttered lines, she filled the whole bay with the dignity of her personality. We dipped our ensign as we passed, and she acknowledged the salute. For weeks to come she covered our decks with soot from her galley fires, for she baked the bread, or so it was said, for the whole of the Navy Base.

As we came alongside a row of officers, drawn up for some reason quite unconnected with us opposite a Navy transport, turned about and faced us, and the senior officer, wearing a sword, took a pace to his front and gave us a formal salute. We felt very undressed for such a ceremonial reception, and I could only answer with a low bow. As soon as we were tied up to the quay, another officer came up and introduced himself as Lieutenant Soulodre, and from then on we became one of his problems, for most of the problems in the Arsenale eventually devolved on him. He became a Commandante while we were there, and as far as we were concerned, we thought that no promotion could have been more justly earned.

He was always well turned out and always charming. He had a broad intelligent face, and his eyebrows met over his nose, partly because they grew that way and partly because he was usually puzzling over one of his problems. If a submarine couldn't dive, or a bow had to be straightened, or a dock gate leaked, or a floating crane was aground, everyone came to Soulodre. For the next few months we were going to bother him with all kinds of questions, and when he saw us a mildly harassed look would come over his face, but he usually stood his ground, if it was obvious that we were making directly for him. Fortunately he spoke English well, although I don't think that he liked to do so.

'Are you ready to be picked out now?' he asked, 'because we'll be able to do it in a few moments.'

We set to work to get the jurymasts down, and it only took a few minutes before they were down on the deck and the rigging stowed. As soon as we'd finished Lieutenant Soulodre returned.

'I am sorry now,' he said, 'the crane has broken down, but it is of no matter because we shall use the floating crane, but it must be at nine o'clock tomorrow morning because of the tide. I am only sorry that you will have to stay another night on the yacht. Tomorrow when we put the yacht on shore you will have to take everything out, and we will have to try and store it somewhere.'

'Can you lend us some packing cases, and fix a place for us to stow it?'

'I will do my best.' Lieutenant Soulodre's best was usually very effective.

For the last time for many months we slept on board *Tzu Hang*. In the morning we were towed round to another wall by two sailors in a rowing boat. A large floating crane was already in position and a bed had been made for *Tzu Hang*'s keel on the dock wall. There was no sign of any spreaders, and there was no time to arrange them, but we were assured by the crew of the crane that she would suffer no damage from the slings, which they padded with sacks. Owing to our lack of Spanish we were very much in their hands, and all we could do was to pretend we were as cool and unperturbed as possible. The slings were adjusted, the crane began to clank and puff and hiss, and *Tzu Hang* was hauled crudely and crookedly out of the water. She hung above our heads, and in our imagination seemed to grow thin before our startled eyes from the pressure of the slings. Her rail bent and there were some loud cracks from the capping. We could see that her hull was clean, with only a few goose-barnacles growing here and there, but there were some ugly scars on the port side aft, where the broken mizzenmast had gouged her. The crane swung her in over her bed and then let her down in a series of runs and jerks, until at last she was laid gently on her bed, undamaged except for a cracked rail capping. After she had been shored up and wedged I noticed that she was leaning slightly to one side.

'*Muy bueno*,' someone laughed, 'she's leaning the right way, against the winter gales.'

I laughed too, but I wouldn't have thought it funny, if I hadn't believed that we would be in the water before the winter gales were really blowing. Months later when north-westerly gales blew down the channel and buffeted her savagely while we worked inside, we used to think comfortably that we were leaning in towards them.

As soon as we were safely ashore a tractor arrived towing a trailer loaded with packing cases, and we set to work to unload the ship, wiping all the tins over with a greasy rag before we stowed them. While we were at work a blue jeep drew up near us, and a grey-headed, slightly built man stepped out. He seemed deceptively gentle as he came towards us, and he greeted us almost diffidently. 'I'm Islay Young,' he said, 'Tanny's brother-in-law.' He had light-blue eyes, steely blue they could be, I thought, when I looked at his determined mouth and chin. He was one of the most liked and respected commanders, when he was on the active list, and sometimes one of the most feared too, and he was a legend now. He had commanded the two sailing ships of the Navy before the *Esmeralda*, and one of them he had sailed round the Horn from east to west. 'I never allowed sail to be taken in without reference to me, when I was below decks,' he told me once, 'but every officer of the watch always knew that he could put sail on.'

He turned to Beryl now and said, 'I think that I was commanding the Navy Base, when you were here just before the war, but I don't think that I had the pleasure of meeting you, not true?'

'Oh, then I must've got a pair of Chilean navy trousers from you. I wore them for ages.'

'Well, not from me, from the stores, not true? I came to tell you,' he went on, 'that I am most sorry that I shall be away for a few weeks, but when 1 return you must all come and stay with me. Jack, Tanny's eldest boy, lives just over the hill there, and he is going to look after you for the time being.'

'But that's all an awful nuisance for you; we wanted to find a flat or a house we could hire somewhere near the dockyard if possible, because we'll be here for a month or so.'

'Well, actually there really aren't any available, but anyway it's quite out of the question. We couldn't hear of it. You are going to stay with us.' He spoke with the authority of the quarterdeck for his own family in their house by the water, on the southern shore of the Boca Chica, for Tanny, in her rambling house on the hills above, and for Jack, in the little sheltered valley, over the hill behind the Arsenale.

The arrival of *Tzu Hang* was quite an event in the Arsenale, and a constant stream of workmen and ratings bent on various tasks and errands found that their shortest way was the circuitous route, which led them along the sea wall and past *Tzu Hang*. The biggest draw was the blue-eyed cat, and her fame spread quickly through the base. They found soon that if they miaowed in imitation of a cat, she ran and peered down at them from the rail, and although Pwe soon tired of it, all afternoon there was a stream of self-conscious and miaowing seamen walking past the ship. Just in front of us on the wall another wooden ship was being rebuilt, frame by frame and plank by plank. She was called *La Fortuna* and the carpenters at work on her were the most enthusiastic of the miaowers, and soon spoilt the market for the others, but they all became our good friends during the time we stood side by side on the sea wall.

We were finished in time for our boxes to be taken away and put into storage, and soon after six o'clock, when the Arsenale had closed down, and the green train which takes the throng of workers on a free ride to Talcahuano town had puffed away on the edge of the road which runs along the bay shore, Jack arrived with his truck to transport us to his home.

The truck climbed the steep cobbled road to a village nearly a thousand feet above the harbour, and Jack stopped for a moment so that we could look down into the bay. There was *Latorre* with her four great mooring chains, and there were the grey rows of corvettes, minesweepers, and landing craft, moored stern on to the quays, whose maintenance gave Lieutenant Soulodre so many problems; and amongst them all was our own particular problem, a small white spot amongst the grey. We drove down a winding gravel road into a valley, to a house with a tennis-court, by a grove of eucalyptus trees. It was all very peaceful after the rush of the day.

When we unpacked the box of clothes from the forecabin, we found that Oscar had helped himself to all my new Australian drip-dry shirts, and to a selection of Beryl's dresses. He had picked only the best. There are rogues on every waterfront, but I think that Oscar was something different, a *specialité du maison*.

Next day a telegram arrived from Clio. 'Gosh I miss all the fun,' it said. 'Isn't *Tzu Hang* wonderful.'

CHAPTER ELEVEN

REPAIRS IN TALCAHUANO

'How long do you think it will take to repair *Tzu Hang*?' we asked
Lieutenant Soulodre.

'I think that we should be able to do it in three weeks, because
the Admiral has said that we must go ahead with it. But first I
must have the drawings for the repairs; and as for a hollow mast,
we have not yet made a hollow mast for a yacht.'

'John will build the masts, and the doghouse, the hatches, and
the woodwork for the rudder, if he has time, but we will want
repairs doing inside, the hull painting, a complete engine overhaul,
and various other things such as the rudder fittings.'

'You will have to make me a list of all that you require, and
the drawings, and then estimates will be prepared by the various
departments. But before any work is done it will be necessary to
pay a deposit to cover the estimates. We have to conform to those
regulations because we do a lot of civilian work here.'

'What about the wood for the masts, the rudder, and the doghouse?'

'All material you will have to buy outside the Arsenale. The
wood for the doghouse should be *lingue* and the wood for the

rudder should be *roble*, but we haven't any wood for the masts. We have some scaffolding planks of Oregon pine in the Arsenale, and perhaps I can arrange for some of those to be made available.'

John spent the next few days searching for wood, and in making his drawings, but he could find no seasoned wood anywhere. Beryl and I were not certain how far the kindness of the authorities in the Navy Base would extend, but we drew up a list of everything from overhauling the engine to the repair of the typewriter.

While we were waiting for the estimates, we transferred from Jack's sun-drenched home behind Talcahuano to Tanny's rambling house, high on the hill above the Boca Chica, surrounded by groves of eucalyptus and pine, and a burnt downland of pasture, cut by deep bush-filled gorges running down to the sea. Here we transported the wood for the doghouse, and John started work, while Beryl and I, when we could get a lift, went down to Talcahuano, and began to clean up in *Tzu Hang*.

Our arrival at Tumbez, as the big old house was called, coincided with the end of the apple season, and every room and corridor in the house, except the living-room, was piled high with apples, with narrow footpaths leading between precariously balanced mounds of Coxes and Kings, and any night voyage was apt to set off a thunderous avalanche of apples, cascading across floors and down stairs.

Tanny was an addict of drama, preferably real drama, such as fire or flood or revolution, but if these were not available, her roving eye searched far and wide for anything that would tickle her sense of the dramatic. She found excitement in the daily race to find an egg as soon as a hen cackled. If the cook got there first, which she often did, because she was as alert as Tanny and often nearer the hen, Tanny was convinced that she had stolen the egg.

153

When all else failed she turned to the cat. 'Your cat has attacked my maid,' she announced one day, her dark eyes sparkling. 'They are terrified of it,' she went on, 'and it growls at them and chases them out of the room.' But she was delighted with the idea of a cat as class-conscious as she was herself.

Tumbez, lovely and serene though it was, was too far away from Talcahuano, and although Tanny, with typical Chilean hospitality, pressed us to stay as long as we liked, we wanted some flat or house, nearer to the Arsenale. One day we met Edward Cooper, who had a business in Talcahuano, and who motored down each day from his home in Concepcion. Edward's father had been British Consul in Chile for fifty years, and Edward, although born in Chile, had been sent to school in England. He had returned to Chile just before the war, and when it broke out he had gone back to England and joined the Navy, as so many others of the British community had done. If he had had a rubber stamp on his forehead, 'Public School and Navy', it couldn't have been more obvious than his clothes, his tie, and his restrained manner proclaimed. It was as if a roc had swooped on Throgmorton Street, picked up a businessman at a venture, and had dropped him in the office in Talcahuano, with its narrow dusty road outside, in a perpetual state of being about to be repaired.

Soon after we had met he asked us if we would like to stay with him during the rest of our time in Chile, at his home in Concepcion.

'Good heavens,' Beryl said, 'you may be letting yourself in for more than you know.'

'No,' he said, 'I have the house and the maids, and it really does them good to have someone to look after besides myself. They get bored.'

'But it might turn into quite a long stay. Two or three months.'

'That's all right. And I'll be able to run you down to Talcahuano each morning in the car, but I can't bring you back. There's an old retainer in the office that I always drop at his home on the way back. But still you'll be able to get back by bus.'

'Then we have a cat.'

'I have a cat too. A ginger tom. I expect that he'll relish a visitor.'

It was arranged that after we'd stayed with Admiral Young, we should move up to Concepcion and live with Edward in the Avenida Pedro Valdivia and this was to become our home while we remained in Chile.

One morning I found Lieutenant Soulodre superintending the docking of a submarine at one end of the dry docks. As soon as he had a moment to spare I asked him how things were going.

'Today it is bad,' he said. 'I have the estimates.'

'How bad?'

'Oh, very bad. They are too much. Far too much. We must go to the office. *Vamos.*'

On the arrival at the office he showed me the figure, and it was almost as much as we had paid for *Tzu Hang*.

'Good heavens!' I said, appalled at the sight of it. 'But we are going to do practically all the carpentry ourselves. We can't possibly pay all that, and all the wood we have to buy outside anyway.'

'Still perhaps we can do something about it. Now you see this for the *carena*, too much, you must do it yourselves. And for this overhaul of the engine, too much, I will see the officer in charge of the transportation section and perhaps we can arrange something. And for this, too much, you must get it done outside. And for this, outside. And for this, it's altogether too expensive here, you must have it done outside. And for this repair of the cabin below decks, it would be much better if you did it all yourselves. Now you see how much we have managed to cut it. It is only half the amount now.'

The fond illusion I had been entertaining of getting something done for nothing faded as quickly as usual, but I was still horrified at the expense. 'But all we've done is to transfer the work from "inside" to this beastly "outside". It will still have to be paid for. Really all we are paying for here is the haul out and the hire of the ground she's standing on. And there are only six pieces of Oregon and we need twelve, and then of course this engine overhaul is more than the cost of the engine when it was new.'

Lieutenant Soulodre was really distressed at the cost, but he was caught up in the usual conflict between the wish to do something outside the regular run, and the restrictions imposed by red tape. 'Well,' he said, 'I think that you will have to speak to Admiral Young. He will be able to arrange something.'

As soon as Admiral Young returned, we went off to see him, and he came with us next day to the office. He left us outside and went in and when he returned he showed us a revised estimate, which was better suited to our means, but as far as I could make out the estimate, for which I had to make a deposit, bore little relation to the bill which might actually be presented at the end of the work.

'It is best not to enquire too much, not true?' said the Admiral. 'Perhaps it would become more expensive.'

'But there are only six pieces of Oregon, and we want twelve.'

'I think that perhaps we may get some more, but we must wait and see, not true?'

With this anxious and nebulous financial arrangement we had to keep our fingers crossed and our hopes on the Admiral. The actual cost of the haul out and hire of the ground on which *Tzu Hang* now stood was no more than we would have expected in any North American port. The cost of all material was high, and the cost of labour was altogether out of our reach. During our stay we had a great deal of assistance in all kinds of work, both officially approved, and unofficially, but we never knew whether a record was kept, and whether we were being charged or not. We followed the Admiral's advice and didn't enquire too much, but the list of odd jobs that we had done, the 'could you just fix this for me?' kind of job, grew and grew. It was a hair-raising business and it was not until we left that we found a lot of the work had been 'overlooked'.

Our next problem was the rudder-post and fittings. There was no bronze rod or bar available in the Arsenale of sufficient diameter to make a new rudder-post. Lieutenant Soulodre told us that our best bet was to try the big coal-mine of Shwager's at Coronel. In this coal kingdom, whose shafts spread for miles under the sea, there were all kinds of material stored, and they were supposed to be able to do almost anything in their shops. I went to the manager's office. He was an Englishman, a strong and incisive character. He looked at the drawings and said, 'I don't think that we have bronze of that type here. The only thing we can do is to make you a steel shaft, coated with bronze. Anyway Bob Smith, the engineer in charge of all the shops, is away. When he gets back you can see him. Anything we can do for you we will do. Cost price.'

Beryl and I didn't like the idea of a bronze-coated steel post, thinking that electrolysis would get to work somewhere, and for the time being we forgot about the facilities that had been offered us at Coronel.

Every day now we were at work once more on *Tzu Hang*. The engine had been taken out at the same time as she was put on the shore, and we set about cleaning her from stem to stern, starting with the bilges. During this time we stayed with Admiral and Señora Young, in their lovely house by the beach. Whenever a Navy ship entered or left the bay, they always closed the shore and blew a salute on their whistle, and the Admiral and his Señora, or Cecilia, his daughter, for he did have a daughter, would run out to acknowledge it, by waving a tablecloth or a sheet. Cecilia was as vigorous as her father, and she could launch a boat in the surf like a fisher-boy. 'You should see the way she handles a boat,' John said, 'and she never lets me row.'

When the Admiral went into Talcahuano in his jeep, he drove at a furious speed, but usually no policeman would dream of stopping him. It happened once when I was with him, but the Admiral handled the poor mistaken man gently. 'He is a new man … a fool,' he said to me afterwards, but I think that in his mind he had lashed him to the mast and ordered his punishment. As he flashed through the Navy Base, although he had retired ten years ago, he was saluted by all the officers and sailors. He was immensely respected by everyone, except perhaps the women of his house. Like Nelson, he did not always seem to have them fully under control.

The Admiral gave me *Cape Horn* by Felix Riesenberg. As I read it I felt my pulse quicken, and I couldn't read it for long, as I found it too disturbing. I thought that I had every intention of taking *Tzu Hang* the easy way up through the Panama Canal, and into the warm weather and the trade wind seas, but perhaps it wasn't so.

One day I heard Beryl say to the Admiral: 'Which way would you go back to England, Islay? Through Magellan or up through the Panama?'

'Well, of course, I should go through Magallanes, but then I should do it at the right time of year, not true? Actually I think that you have less wind in the Channels in the winter than in the summer, but then you have so much darkness, so I think that the best time is to go down at the end of the summer or at the end of the winter. Now would be a good time for example, or in

October. Of course your husband should really see the Patagonian Channels, it is a new world, not true? And then you would be in sheltered water all the way.'

'Do you hear that?' she said. 'Do you hear what Islay says?'

'Yes, I heard, but I thought that you didn't want to go down the Channels, because they're so cold and wet. At least that's what I've always heard before.'

'Not always,' the Admiral said. 'Not always. Sometimes there is beautiful weather. But you can't say that you've seen Chile, until you have seen the Canales, not true?'

'Anyway I don't want to go beating into the Caribbean against the trade wind,' said Beryl.

As the doghouse and hatches took shape on Admiral Young's verandah, for we had moved all the carpentry with us, Beryl and I continued our scrubbing and cleaning in the Navy yard. As we worked we found all sorts of odd things lodged in the strangest of places, but we never found the hatchet which we always kept in a canvas pocket by the side of the cook's seat in the galley, and immediately below the hatch. It had been sadly missed during the days after the smash, when we needed it badly to split up wood for the fire. We had always assumed that it was under the engine, the only inaccessible spot in the ship, but now that the engine was out we could find no trace of it, and the only reasonable assumption was that it had gone out of the hatch when we were upside down. It was another indication of what had happened to us, but we were to find more graphic proof, when Beryl started to clean out the forecabin.

One day she called me forward and pointed to the deckhead by the bulkhead at the end of her berth. 'Look at that,' she said.

'What on earth is it?'

'It's my tin of face powder.'

Squeezed between the top of the bulkhead and the deckhead and squashed absolutely flat, part of a small round tin protruded from the bulkhead. A pinkish powder, set in a hard paste, had been squeezed out of it.

'It was in the shelf there,' she said, pointing to a shelf at the head of her berth, and to a small partition in the shelf, which was immediately below the tin. 'How on earth did it get stuck in there?'

'Good Lord! It must've happened when we turned over … in a somersault as you said. It could've only happened like that. As we went upside down the tin must've slid down the bulkhead to the deckhead, and then when the masts began to go, the twin forestays pulled this deck-beam up and cracked it, and lifted the deck, so that the tin slipped in between the deck and the bulkhead, and the moment the mast broke, the deck snapped back and caught it.'

'I vote we leave it there, because we can only dig it out with a chisel, and no one is going to believe it if we take it away. It's really the best proof of what happened.' So we left it there.

The weeks passed quickly even if the progress on *Tzu Hang* was slow. The doghouse and hatches were finished and installed, and the new perspex lights and the windows were fitted. The doghouse was a beautiful job of lower and more graceful design than the old one, with its corners dovetailed, and strong corner posts cross-bolted into the deck-beams and carlins. To Beryl and me it was a miracle of carpentry, but John started to worry about the wood, which began to check as it dried. 'But you won't lose that one,' he promised us.

We had written to England for some mast-track and to a friend in Panama for some resorcinol resin glue for the mast. Meanwhile John turned his attention to the rudder.

We were well into the Chilean winter and *Tzu Hang* was snug once more. Every day the three of us would eat our lunch on board, while the fire burnt without smoking in the stove, and across the football ground a loudspeaker blared Spanish tunes for the entertainment of the dockyard workers during their lunch hour. The musty smell of dampness and mould and dirty bilges had gone from *Tzu Hang*, and now there was the clean smell of paint and wood shavings.

The change of John's activities from doghouse and skylights to the rudder marked a new period in our fortunes in Chile. It marked the period of Señor Martinez as opposed to the period of Lieutenant, now Commandante, Soulodre. Soulodre was in charge of most of the things that went on in the Arsenale, and with the exception of the Automobile Section, Señor Martinez seemed to be in charge of all the rest. Commandante Soulodre had the docks, the cranes, the panel beaters, the forge, the welders, the huge machines that sliced up armourplate, and most of the noisemakers; Señor Martinez was in charge of the big carpenters' shop, with all the wood-working machines, and the Taller de Botes, where all the small boats of the fleet were repaired. Whereas Commandante Soulodre seemed to be oppressed by the weight of his responsibility, Señor Martinez bore his as lightly as a feather. He was a civilian employee in the Arsenale, and he gave the impression of being a man of considerable means, who had accepted this employment to gratify a hobby.

Señor Martinez' moustache was shaved to a narrow line above his lip, and his eyebrows were almost permanently raised as if in surprise or mild disdain. He was always impeccably dressed, and he walked through his shops leaving a delicate whiff of scent, like a vapour trail, behind him. If ever he touched a clean piece of wood, he dusted the tips of his fingers together afterwards, and then wiped them with a spotless handkerchief. I never saw him touch a dirty piece. He refused to attempt English and regarded my attempts at Spanish with ill-concealed disgust, and once, after I had polished up and made a short speech, in what I thought was excellent Spanish, he handed me a dictionary and said, 'You really must speak Spanish.' When Beryl approached him in her old paint-stained dungarees and a cloth tied round her hair, he leant towards her courteous and attentive; it was fascinating to watch him, perfectly groomed, a quizzical and almost affectionate look on his face, while she showered him with her nouns and infinitives.

Whereas I regarded Commandante Soulodre as my especial friend and confidant, to whom I applied for assistance, Beryl was quite enchanted by Señor Martinez, who was no less than astounded by her. She could get anything that she wanted out of him. John made no requests from anyone, but now that the scene of his work, in the Señor Martinez period, was transferred to the Taller de Botes, the quality of his work made him master of all the carpenters there. Unasked for he had all the help he required, and he used only three words: 'Good' and 'Not good'.

The Señor Martinez period also coincided with our transfer to Concepcion, and to the luxury of Edward's house in the Avenida Pedro Valdivia, a luxury that we hadn't experienced since before the war, and are never likely to experience again. The house was ruled by Carmen, an old maid who had served Edward's family for fifty years. She regarded us all as children, and Edward she referred to as 'Eduardito'. He told us that she could be as stubborn as a mule if she was crossed. Lydia was the lame little cook, as jolly as a sparrow, who provided matchless meals without discussion, who always opened the gates for the car in the morning, and waved a coy goodbye. Teresa, usually known as 'the little girl', was the general handmaid. 'The little girl' was a thorn in Edward's side, but she went with Lydia, and was therefore indispensable. She waited at table, and always nudged us if we didn't notice that she was waiting to serve us, with a thump like a mule's kick, and after she had put the plates with the bird pattern on the table, she used to run round, clicking her tongue, and spinning the plates round, so that the heads of the birds all faced inwards. We all thought that Edward's problem of her employment might be solved if she married the gardener, and at times there did seem to be signs of a budding romance.

From now on, leaving the cat in the care of Carmen, Lydia, and Teresa, we went every morning to Talcahuano with Edward, returning every evening by bus, and when we got back the shabby unwanted girl flowered under Beryl's kindness, and told her long stories about the adored cat, '*con los ojos azules*'. The ginger tom fought every night to ensure that he had first rights when the time came, but he knew nothing about modern operations, and the cat remained as virginal, and as wayward, as when she arrived.

We used to leave the Arsenale at about six o'clock in the evening, with numbers of naval ratings, also bound for Concepcion. Just as the attaché case in England is the badge of the commuting business-man, so the attaché case in Chile is the badge of the commuting sailor. Every morning they came flocking into the Arsenale, fat sailors, thin sailors, clean-shaven or surprisingly moustached, with their attaché cases and hurried steps, and every evening they hurried out again to make long queues for the Concepcion buses. Beryl, John and I would avoid the queue by walking half a mile in the wrong direction and catching the bus at the Torpedo Base, where it started, and thereby getting a seat instead of standing room only. In all the months of these daily journeys in crowded buses we met with nothing but good manners, and the worst that we had ever to put up with was the breath of a convivial traveller, loaded with red wine and garlic.

By now two months had passed and John was ready to start on the masts. Señor Martinez allotted him a large space in the Taller de Botes to lay out a bed for them, and he went to select the wood from the store of scaffolding planks. When he came back he shook his head: 'Pretty crummy,' he said. 'There's a knot every foot, but I suppose that it's the best we can do. We'll have to stagger the knots. They're all quite firm anyway.'

After some difficulty we were able to get another six long planks of Oregon, and we then had sufficient for the masts and booms. We were thankful enough to get it, as it was all imported and apparently the only Oregon to be had anywhere. But now we began to be anxious about the special glue that we had sent for and which had arrived in the country weeks before. We had not got the right touch with the Customs officials, and it began to look as if we would never get it out of the shed. We were also exasperated by another set-back which had nothing to do with the Customs. The mast-track had been sent from England addressed to us in Talcahuano, on a ship calling at Valparaiso and Talcahuano. It was off-loaded at Valparaiso instead of Talcahuano, and when it was found and sent on by the next ship, it was overlooked and returned to Valparaiso. 'But that's nothing,' we were told, 'you'll be jolly lucky if it's not shipped back to England.' It arrived in the end, long after John had gone and the masts were made, and months after it had first arrived in Chile. We began to wonder just how long the other shipments from London would take, and if they would ever arrive in time for us to get away with them in the spring.

We had also been unable to solve the problem of the rudder-post, but we were getting nearer a solution. One day we had seen Commandante Soulodre on the prowl in the docks near *Tzu Hang*, and had tackled him again.

'What you really want,' he said, 'is a rolled bronze propeller-shaft.'

'Well, what about that?' Beryl asked, pointing to the shaft of an old launch nearby, lying on the side of the dock.

'That would do fine,' he said, 'but I don't know who is in charge of these old boats. I'll try and find out and get permission.'

Some weeks later we saw Commandante Soulodre and Señor Martinez talking together near the same old launch. We tackled them again. 'I have told them that we could turn down a rudder-post for them out of that propeller-shaft,' said the Commandante, 'but I can't find out who owns it.'

'My dear fellow, that's mine,' said Señor Martinez. 'Of course you can have it. Do whatever you like with it, only don't for heavens sake say I said so.' I don't think that he had ever seen the launch before.

A few days afterwards the propeller was taken off, and then workmen came periodically to struggle with the coupling until it was cut with an oxy-acetylene flame, and the shaft was taken away to the submarine base, the only place with a lathe long enough to fit it. While this was going on the rudder fittings were cast and fitted, and the glue arrived at last from the Customs, suddenly, with a rush, and there was nothing to pay.

It was mid-winter. The westerly gales blew great curtains of rain across the harbour, and lashed *Tzu Hang* so that, while we worked inside her, it was possible to imagine that we were at sea again. The wind rattled the closed doors of the Taller de Botes and chased the shavings about inside as we slid them apart a fraction to go in or come out, and it ruffled the feathers of the seagulls which sought shelter on the sandy football pitch behind *Tzu Hang*. Thousands of cormorants, down from Peru in search of food, struggled low across the water looking for shelter, and all along the rocky beach on the way to the Admiral's house they stood in forlorn and disconsolate groups.

One of the problems that the cold weather brought us was how we should get enough heat to make the glue for the masts set up. In the Taller de Botes the temperature went down into the forties, and we needed a temperature of 70° Fahrenheit for several hours. After failing to find any suitable method in the Arsenale, I went over to Coronel to talk to Bob Smith.

Bob is another bluff and uncompromising Yorkshireman, and he was then in charge of all mechanical maintenance above ground in this vast concern of Shwager's. But on top of being in charge of the technical maintenance of the mine, he was heavily involved in a big face-lifting process that was going on, and he was very short of trained engineers. 'I keep training them and some other outfit buys them,' he told me later. 'You can't expect them to stay if they can get better wages elsewhere.' To be trained by, or to have worked under, Bob Smith, served as a special diploma.

He was looking over plans, a slide-rule in his hand and his long-distance glasses pushed up on his forehead, when I found him. I came to think of Bob and his slide-rule together, like a double-barrelled name. He could probably tell how much beer he could drink in half an hour without reference to it, but it seemed to appear from his pocket for almost any other problem. There were three men in his office, and when the last came out I went in. 'You want to become one of Bob's lost causes,' a friend had told me, 'and when you're one of his causes you're home and dry.' I didn't know how to become a cause with this grey-eyed man, who stared at me coldly through a haze of tobacco smoke. He wasn't giving anything away. I told him my name and said that I hoped he'd be able to do something for me.

'Everyone wants something done for them,' he said, 'it all depends what you want, and what you've got, mate,' he said.

I told him about the yacht.

'Oh yes,' he said, 'the Boss told me about you. You got into a kind of a mess, didn't you? Now what do you want?'

I told him about the mast and our heating problems.

'What you want are some infra-red bulbs and you could string them along the mast, and then you'd have to erect some sort of tent over them. They'd give you enough heat. What's the length of the mast? Have you got a power plug where you're building it? Right, I'll get you fifty lamps—they're ordinary brooder lamps—and have them wired up for you. Anything else you want?'

'Yes. I want 200 10-inch bolts for wooden clamps to clamp the mast together when we glue it.'

'No problem,' he said, 'we can turn those out in very short order. I'll let you have those tomorrow, as there's certain to be a truck going in to Concepcion. You can let us have the whole lot back when you've finished with them as we can always use them. No charge for those. Now come along to the club and have a drink, otherwise I'll get stuck in this bloody office all night.'

Before we left the club Bob told me to bring any other problems to him and I began to hope that *Tzu Hang* might become one of his causes. We came to know that 'No problem' well and it smoothed out many creases.

The scaffolding planks that we were able to get from the Arsenale were 36 feet by 10 inches by 2 inches. In order to use single planks for the mizzen we cut it down to 36 feet, which was a foot shorter than the design we had drawn. We had decided to shorten the whole rig, to do away with *Tzu Hang*'s bowsprit, and to have just a single headsail, so that she would be easier to handle for the two of us alone. But that was not the only reason, for the fact of the matter was that we were beginning to think, tentatively and rather timorously, of another shot at the south. The mainmast was reduced to 47 feet above the deck, and a little more than 54 feet over all.

The first task was to glue the scarves of the several lengths of planking that were to make the mainmast. We made a long tent over the planks from spare sails and some tarpaulins, strung up our lights and switched on the heat, and the temperature rose sufficiently for the glue to set firmly. The planks had already been machine-planed in the workshop, but John decided that they were not fair enough to be glued together, and the whole had to be hand-planed again. Next he traced out the lines of the masts and cut the planks to shape with a small electric hand-saw that we were able to borrow from the carpenters' shop.

There were four planks for the mizzen and four lengths, scarfed together, for the main, and as soon as they were cut to shape, we started on the gluing. John was in charge and Beryl and I were his two apprentices. First two lengths were glued together, and covered with newspaper so that the next lot didn't stick to them. Then the next two lengths, the other half of the mast, were glued and laid on top. Then they were all clamped together, by bolting wooden clamps along the whole length of the mast. We started with the mizzenmast, cooking it in its long coffin-like tent for eight hours, but as sometimes the lights went out and because we couldn't keep them on after hours, it was always two days before we dared consider that the glue was safely set. The two halves of each mast were then hollowed by hand, and then glued together in the final operation. While the glue was setting, John prepared the booms which also had to be glued. All the major carpentry was now finished except for the final planing and shaping of the masts, and what remained to be done, the spinnaker booms and the dinghy, we would have made 'outside'.

It was time for John to leave. He explained carefully how the masts should be shaped and made templates for us to check our planing, but he obviously had grave doubts as to whether we were capable of doing it correctly ... and so had we. He had been so long with us and had put so much of his skilled time and work into *Tzu Hang*, that it was hard to think of her without him. He seemed to be one of us and part of *Tzu Hang*. We had been through a great adventure together, and we knew the worst and the best of each other. When he left us we felt strangely forlorn.

CHAPTER TWELVE

STILL IN TALCAHUANO

Four months had gone since we had arrived in Chile. It seemed almost impossible that four months could have gone and yet so much remain to be done. John had stayed on longer than he had intended at first, to accomplish less. As well as the dinghy and the spinnaker booms, there remained to be done all the mast and boom fittings, all the rigging, the pulpit and the rails, and the mainsail had to be altered to fit the shortened mast. On top of this a large shipment of sails and rope, blocks and stainless steel wire, and all kinds of other things was still to be sent from England, and now that we knew something of the hazards of delay and theft through which it would have to pass on its way out, we began to wonder how much we would see of it, and whether it would arrive in time.

The officers and men in the Arsenale, with whom we came in contact, did all that they could to help us, but what work they did was done more or less unofficially, in between official jobs. We couldn't press them too hard, as we never knew whether we were being charged for the work or not, and anyway we were visitors in a foreign land and had to be patient. Yet they didn't like to disappoint us and to say that something couldn't be done. It was always just a question of time, and time meant so much to us, who were so anxious to get away, and so little to them. The Admiral had said that we should leave in October, before the southerly wind blew strongly and while we might still get a wind from the north to help us south. Then too we would find less wind in the Channels, and it was of the south and the Channels that were we thinking now.

Late October or November is a good time for going north too. The southerly winds are beginning, and they would take us north to the south-east trades, and we would have a fair wind and current to the Equator. We could be through the Panama Canal by Christmas, and we could spend the rest of the northern winter in the West Indies, and be home by June or July. It was the easiest, the most sensible, and the most attractive route to take, but it would be a confession of failure—that was the crux of the matter—and we didn't like to make it.

All the same, when I woke up in the night and heard the wind hooting round the corners and buffeting the windows of the secure and comfortable house in which we lived, I felt a sense of foreboding as I thought of those big and lonely seas further south. I felt as if I was being driven by something out of my control, unresisting and yet unwilling, towards a fate that I had to face. These gloomy thoughts were sometimes interrupted by an impish whisper which seemed to say that the something out of my control was Beryl. I don't think it was. She had the same feeling too.

One of the reasons for our slow progress was the difficulty that we had in speaking Spanish. Beryl, who tackles almost any language without shame, achieved wonders with her French-German-Spanish *patois*, and to see her talking, her hands flying in all directions, so that her audience winced away from her, was to believe that she was a fluent linguist. Sometimes, at a cocktail party or a dinner, she would be surrounded by people, each with an eager, alert, and slightly puzzled look. I have seen the same expression on the face of a Scotch sheepdog which had been bought recently by a Norfolk shepherd. But even Beryl's ingenuity with languages couldn't overcome the difficulty of explaining some yacht fitting that we required, and often we understood that something was actually being done for us, when we had really been told that it was hoped that it would be done, sometime in the future.

Another reason for the delay was that we had no means of transport, and had to go everywhere by microbus. In spite of the furious driving of the bus drivers, this was a slow and exasperating way of getting about, and we wasted a prodigious amount of time in the bus queues. *Diós es mi Co-piloto* was a favourite slogan, written up on the roof above the driver's head, and they drove with such assurance and apparent negligence, that it did seem as if they thought that He was in the co-driver's seat, and at least in partial control. As they drove side by side down the road, in a desperate race to get ahead of each other to steal the passengers at the next bus-stop, they bowed and crossed themselves at the scenes of previous accidents, marked by little altars and burning candles at the side of the road. We became as hardened and inured to danger as the other passengers, and it was only when we saw them crossing themselves too, that we realised we were up against it.

'*¿No le gusta Chile?*' they used to ask.

'*Mucho gusta.*'

'Aren't you glad you came?'

'Very glad.'

'Could you have come to a better place?'

'We couldn't have come to kinder people,' we used to say, but in fact, from the point of view of fitting out a yacht, Chile was not a good place to come to, because there was no yachting industry there. Owing to import restrictions it was difficult to find much that we wanted, and the sort of equipment that was available was appropriate for iron-hulled fish-boats and rarely suitable for a yacht.

We wore out our shoes and our tempers trudging round and round the shops of Talcahuano and Concepcion, in endless pursuit of some substitute for the many things that we wanted, but couldn't get.

Brass hinges were unobtainable, although we could get brass-coated ones, useless for a sea-going ship, and brass screws were always hard to find. We could find a dozen here and a dozen there, and we used to go over them in the shops with a magnet to see that we weren't getting brass-covered ones. The shopkeepers used to join enthusiastically in the sport. Shackles too were scarce until a number of German shackles made an appearance in the shops. They had a suspicious lustre about them, and after a few weeks they were covered in rust.

But our ill-wind brought good to one of the chandlers in Talcahuano, for Beryl brought him luck if ever she visited his shop. 'Señora,' he said, 'please come every morning even if you do not buy. It is a most extraordinary thing that if ever you come in the morning, I have exceptional—*prodigioso*—sales in the afternoon. You are very lucky, Señora.'

Next day I asked him what effect Beryl's visit had had.

'*Fantástico*,' he said, 'the sales were doubled.'

Beryl began to enjoy this reputation and to hope that there might be something in it which would pay off in the future.

The carpenters on *La Fortuna*, our sister ship on the sea wall, couldn't understand our eagerness to be off. They had a nice job in the open when the sun shone, and they were away from the workshop boss, and could have a pleasant rest and a smoke in a nearby shed when it rained. 'When are you going into the water?' they used to ask us.

'Next month.'

'Never!' they shouted, laughing. 'We're going into the water next month too,' and they patted the old bareboned hulk which had made so little progress since we had arrived. But they were always ready to down tools, and to give us a hand if we needed it, and if they saw Beryl putting up the heavy iron ladder which we used for getting up on to *Tzu Hang*, there would be a scurry of helpers from *La Fortuna*.

One day, when we were all holding a discussion group over one of our problems on board *Tzu Hang*, there was a sudden rush from the deck to the scaffolding on the seaward side. *Fortuna*'s men had turned and gone together, without a word spoken, in an intuitive communal movement, like a flight of dotterel along the seashore. I found them all lying along the planks of the scaffolding.

'What on earth's the matter?' I asked.

'It's the Admiral,' they hissed. 'He's inspecting the dockyard.'

One by one they dropped down to the ground, still keeping under cover, until they were once more, although for the first time that day, hard at work on *La Fortuna*. From where we were, it looked as if the Admiral, then in charge of the whole naval establishment in Talcahuano, was inspecting the old Admiral's launch, and wondering perhaps what had happened to the propeller-shaft.

In spite of all this friendly assistance there were days when we felt we were living in a nightmare, where nothing was ever quite finished, where people never said exactly what they meant, and where everything that we wanted was just out of reach. Only in the evening did things begin to return to normal, when, after being bent double under the roof of a lurching and crowded bus, Beryl and I used to jump out in the dark and the rain opposite the station, and splash across the street towards the Avenida Pedro Valdivia. Past two smart and ultra-modern taxis, past a row of wretched cabs with poor disconsolate horses, past a crowded wine-shop at a corner, and over a vast uncovered trench in the footpath, until we saw the lights of Edward's house shining warmly through the tall iron railings. Then we used to fumble with cold wet hands for a key, unlock the gate, unlock the door, and there find Carmen waiting to take our coats and clucking at the weather. Then the sitting room door would open, and Edward would say, 'Ah! Just in time for a Pisco sour before your bath.'

On Sundays Edward and Beryl and I would take off into the hills behind Concepcion on long walking expeditions, carrying hot *empanadas*, a Chilean Cornish pasty, wonderfully flavoured, wrapped in a cloth in a basket. The heart of the *empanada*, the very essence of its flavour, was found somewhere near the centre, where an olive ringed by the white of a hard-boiled egg was concealed. Of all the excellent Chilean food the thought of an *empanada* makes my mouth water most, but *locos* and *erizos*, two kinds of shellfish, are dishes for the most fastidious of gourmets. Chilean wine we found excellent too, and cheap, and Pisco, a form of gin but distilled from the grape, made splendid cocktails, either with lemon as a Pisco sour, or with vermouth.

During the winter there was an epidemic of rabies, and the dogcatchers were out around the town in a truck, tossing out small pieces of meat loaded with strychnine for the stray dogs. Even without the poison the mortality in dogs was high, partly due to a disregard for danger by the dogs, a disregard that they shared with many pedestrians, and partly due to the furious driving of the microbuses.

On one of our Sunday walks a small dog came yapping out from behind a hut and bit me in the ankle. I have never been bitten

175

before, except when involved in a dog fight, and I was furiously angry. With a rush of adrenalin and bellowing like a wounded bull, I picked up a stick and threw it at the dog. All the pent up repressions of the past months were released with the stick, but the dog dodged it easily, and it hit Edward instead.

'That dog's not mad,' said Beryl, 'I've never seen anything look so pleased with itself.'

'No, but Miles is,' Edward agreed.

Marta, Jack's beautiful, grey-eyed and shapely wife used to come to the Arsenale sometimes, to give us a hand with the work, and now that spring was on the way, we took advantage of the warmer weather to paint the ship. From the top of the wall where *Tzu Hang* was standing, to the water below her, was about 14 feet. The dock-yard hands were always passing, walking along the top of the wall, especially when Marta was with us. On one of those days Beryl and Marta were alone on the boat, when they heard a splash, and then a terrified wailing: '*!O Mama mía, o Mama mía, ayuda, ayuda!*' The carpenters of *La Fortuna* were running to the rescue before Beryl and Marta had realised what had happened, and they lowered a long scaffolding plank and towed the poor fellow to a ladder.

'What happened, what happened?' Marta called to them.

'He was looking at you,' they said, and doubled up with laughter.

A few days later and while we were still waiting for news of the rudder-post, which had vanished into the submarine base in order to be turned down to the right size, we were painting the masts in the Taller de Botes. While we were painting, Jim Byrne, a solid and hospitable Yorkshireman, who was in business in Concepcion, arrived to see how we were getting on. Jim was always plotting how best he could give us a hand. I don't know whether he spent more time in wondering how he could help us, or in wondering how he could do so without appearing to inconvenience himself.

It is a Yorkshire trait, and we could always see through it. Now he said that as he had had nothing to do, he'd just come down to watch someone else working for a change, but he soon had a paint-brush in his hand, and was grumbling something about 'getting the stick from Moll for the paint on my trousers'.

While he was at work Señor Martinez came floating delicately, and as dapper as ever, through the workshop. 'Do ask him, Jim, how the rudder-post is getting along,' I said, and he was soon buried in conversation with the natty Señor. When he came back to us he was able to tell us all Señor Martinez' difficulties, and how much he was trying to help us and keep the costs down, but what it all boiled down to was that owing to pressure of work in the other departments, he could really only help us with the carpentry. It would be better to take the rudder-post, and all the castings, over to Shwager's at Coronel, and to Bob Smith, who spoke the same language. Without more ado we got the rudder-post, loaded it on to Jim's truck, and set off for Coronel.

We found Bob as usual working in the office long after everyone else had left, and only dimly visible through the cloud of cigarette smoke, which always hung about his table. He listened while I tried to explain what I wanted.

'How are you going to fasten the post to the rudder?' he asked.

'We were going to weld it on to two arms, like this,' I said, and drew him a sketch.

'Well I don't know anything about yachts, but I don't like it,' he said. 'What sort of strain is going to come on the rudder?' and he pulled out his slide-rule.

'Normally not much, but if we were lying to a sea-anchor in a storm it might be pretty considerable. You see there would be about twenty tons of boat drifting backwards, and then there would be the rolling.'

'Well you can't do that, mate,' he said, 'it's against all the bloody principles of welding. You can't put a bloody strain across a long weld like that. It has to be on the line of the weld.' I knew that he would always say exactly what he thought. 'Here,' he went on, 'look here,' and he started drawing in his turn. In the end he had an enormous fitting cast in the shops, through which the rudder-post passed and was then locked in place by a long key. 'There,' he said, after it was made, 'you won't lose that one.'

'And even if the wood goes, we'll still be able to steer with the rudder fitting,' Beryl added.

I drew the plans and diagrams for all the mast and boom fittings and gave them to Bob, and he put his men on to making moulds and castings. The mast-fittings were let out on a contract to one of his engineers, and it was some time before they were completed, as they were hand-made from sheet brass, and it wasn't until the end of September that we had everything back. Meanwhile I had spliced up all the shrouds and stays at their upper ends. I didn't intend to finish them until we had the masts in, and I could measure them under tension, to make certain that they were the right length.

Señor Martinez lent us a carpenter to help us in shaping the ends of the booms to take the fittings, and for drilling the holes through the masts, to take the bolts for the tangs. Neither of us could guarantee that the end of the drill would come out on the other side exactly opposite the point at which it had gone in, if we had tried to do it. The mast-track arrived at last, and we screwed it on and gave the masts another coat of paint, and while they were drying we started to get *Tzu Hang* ready to go into the water again.

After being so long ashore she needed completely recaulking. The caulking compound that we had ordered from America had been held for two months in the Customs, but it was released now, just in time, and we got a professional to do the job. Then we gave her a coat of anti-fouling paint and she was ready for the sea. But before all this happened there had been another change in the Arsenale, which affected our work, and even the surroundings that we had become so accustomed to.

One day, when Beryl and I got out of the car at Talcahuano, we looked across the edge of the bay to the dockyard, as we did every morning, hoping to see *Tzu Hang*'s small white hull perched up on the sea wall. We saw *Tzu Hang*, but we also saw, high above the drab buildings, high above the lines of minesweepers and corvettes moored to the mole, four tall masts. It was the Chilean training ship, *Esmeralda*, who had arrived in the inner harbour, and who now spread the mantle of her grace around her so that there was no one who entered the dockyard gates whose eyes were not lifted in admiration to her tall spars. From then on, when we walked to *Tzu Hang*, we always walked the length of the quay where she was moored. It was as if a relation had appeared in a foreign country, and we felt better for her presence.

She was square-rigged on the foremast only, and did not have all the beauty of a fully square-rigged ship, but she was the most beautiful thing in the harbour, tall and slender. Her arrogant bowsprit soared upwards, and a condor was her figurehead below.

That afternoon, while Beryl and I were working on *Tzu Hang*, we heard a hail from below. We looked over the rail and saw a tall broad-faced man, a captain in the Chilean Navy, calling up to us.

'I'm Bonnafoss,' he said, 'commanding the *Esmeralda*. I wanted to know if there was anything I could do for you?'

He spoke in French. Beryl and I clambered down and shook hands.

'We got in yesterday,' he said, 'and I'm just going off on leave. If you think of any way in which I can help you, I will arrange it before I go. I will see something of you when I come back, and anything else that I can do before you leave we can arrange then.'

'I wonder,' said Beryl, 'if your sailmaker could sew up the mainsail for us. We have had to take out two cloths, and now the lower part of the leach has to be altered, and it all has to be sewn together again.'

'Of course he can. I'll send him along at once.'

Captain Bonnafoss always did exactly what he said he was going to do, and usually earlier than we expected, and a few minutes after his broad back had disappeared round the wharf shed on his way to *Esmeralda*, the sailmaker and his mate arrived. We showed him the pencilled markings that we had made on the sail, and as soon as he understood them, they bundled the sail up and took it away. We thought it very remarkable that the captain of a four-masted training ship should have taken the trouble to walk all the way over to *Tzu Hang* to ask if he could be of some assistance, so soon after coming in and just before going on leave, but Captain Bonnafoss was a very remarkable man.

As soon as *Tzu Hang*'s bottom was painted I went off to make arrangements for the crane to put her into the water.

'At nine o'clock sharp,' said Commandante Soulodre, and he was in a very affable mood. 'At nine o'clock on Friday, and you must be ready then, because of the tide.'

'And could we have some spreaders, so that the rail won't be damaged by the slings.'

'Of course.'

On Friday we were ready at nine o'clock sharp, in fact we were ready an hour before then, because we had persuaded Edward to drive us all the way down to the yacht at eight, but at nine o'clock there was still no crane in sight. I went round to the office in search of the hard-working and long-suffering Commandante, but found that he had been called away suddenly to Santiago, and no one in the office now knew anything about the crane. I was told that I would have to make out a formal application for the crane, which would have to be signed, and that the crane could not possibly be ready on that day. 'But it was all done two days ago,' I said, 'it was all arranged.'

'But never mind, it is quite easy to arrange again; only not today.'

'But tomorrow's Saturday, and then there's Sunday.'

'And after that Monday.'

It had become absurdly important for us to get *Tzu Hang* into the water on that day, it seemed almost symbolic of success. If only she could float again, we felt we would be nearly off. But as in the Chilean winter the sunshine follows the rain, and the flowers bloom at the most unlikely times, now Teniente Fernandez arrived, short and broad and beaming, to say that the crane was actually on its way.

'Have you any spreaders?' I asked him.

'No, no spreaders.'

I ran off breathless in search of Señor Martinez, and the floating crane, a carpenter, and two long baulks of timber arrived at *Tzu Hang* all at the same time.

As soon as the floating crane was in position, with her kedge anchors out and made fast to the wall, Teniente Fernandez came up to us. 'All ready now?' he asked. He was wearing a pair of large leather work-gloves, like a badge of office. The crane swung its hook over *Tzu Hang* and two large wire slings were put into position under the keel. I noticed that one strand had frayed through on one of them, but Teniente Fernandez assured me confidently that they could still pick up twice the weight of *Tzu Hang*. When the slings were in position the carpenter started to fit the spreaders, and before he had finished the whistle blew, and everyone knocked off for lunch. Beryl and I were left once more in a state of fluttering suspension, hardly able to believe that having got so far, it had all stopped again.

During the lunch interval music was played as usual over the loudspeaker system and the tune that came floating across the football ground was *Que será, será*, whatever will be, will be.

'Listen to that damned tune,' I said to Beryl, 'I wonder if we'll have to pay for the extra time.'

After the interval Teniente Fernandez came up to us again. He was as relaxed and cheerful as ever. 'The tide …' he said.

'No, don't tell me.'

'Yes. We've lost it. We will have to wait for a couple of hours.'

We waited for the tide to ebb and to flow, and at five in the evening it was thought to be high enough. *Tzu Hang* was hoisted up into the air, and the props and shores fell away from her hull, but as she went up the floating crane went down and we were soon hard aground.

'Never mind,' said the Teniente, 'we must wait some more.'

The whistles blew again and the dockyard workers started hurrying along the sea wall on their way home, and as if in answer to the same signal the cormorants came flying in long lines out of the bay, on their way to the rocks where they would spend the night. As the men from the yard passed us they wished us a happy night, and Teniente Fernandez, still complacent and unruffled, lit a cigarette, while his crew sought what shelter they could behind the crane from the chilly south wind, which was splashing wave tops on to the deck. *Tzu Hang* remained hanging in her slings, and I thought of the frayed wire rope, and half expected to hear it crack before we got her into the water.

They tried again, and this time the crane began to slide away towards her anchors. For a panicky moment we saw that *Tzu*

Hang's keel was not going to clear an iron bollard on the wall, but she was lifted at the last moment and swung out over the sea, and then with a rush and a splash, in a burst of Chilean élan, she was lowered into the water, where she lay bobbing and bowing to the little waves like a Muscovy duck newly arrived in a pool. She was towed round and made fast near the *Esmeralda*, and when we got home that night, long after dinner-time, Edward had a special amount of Pisco sour ready for us, and we felt as if we needed it.

Now we were ready to put the masts in and again in need of a crane. Señor Martinez was interested in this, as the masts were in his workshop, and he wanted us to use the huge electrically operated crane, which ran on rails along the side of the big dry dock.

'*¿Es muy preciso,*' he said, holding up his hand, his little finger extended and his thumb and forefinger a fraction apart, as if he was drinking a cup of coffee in the most fragile and delicate of cups, 'to the thickness of an eggshell, *no es cierto?*'

But the big crane wasn't available, and I had to go to the donkey crane, at work in one of the smaller dry docks. It also was on rails and could get to us if we moored just outside the dry-dock gates. It didn't look '*muy preciso,*' as it puffed and snorted, heaving huge masses of ironmongery out of the hull of a ship in the dock, but we brought the ship round and made her fast.

In order to get the masts down to the dockside, we needed a trailer and tractor, which Señor Martinez had said that he would arrange, but by midday no masts had arrived. I began to wonder if the crane would be ready before the masts, and went in search of Señor Martinez. I can't imagine what my own reaction would have been in my army days, if two foreigners with a broken-down car had appeared day after day in the regimental lines in search of something or other from the workshops. I suppose it might have been violent, but Señor Martinez and the others had now put up

183

with us for months and their patience had far exceeded any liability that might be claimed as due to the brotherhood of the sea.

Now for the first time I saw him out of humour, but apparently not with me. He flung his arms out with an extravagant gesture and burst into English with a fluency that I had never even suspected. 'It is remarkable,' he said, 'of all the tractors in this Arsenale, not one can I find ... anywhere.' I went off to try and find one myself, and when I returned riding triumphantly on its towing bar, tractors were converging on Señor Martinez from all directions. We got the masts down to the dockside undamaged, and there our relations with Señor Martinez ended, as they had already ended with Commandante Soulodre, no doubt to their relief, but to our lasting regret.

It was not till after the whistle had gone in the evening that the crane arrived, the driver working overtime for no pay on our behalf, and two carpenters had also stayed on, unasked, to help. The masts were picked up in the air while we steadied them, and then each in turn swooped down on the deck with a terrifying clanking, to stop a few inches above the aperture. We guided them in, and then there was another rush as if they were going to be dropped through the bottom of the boat. Then for the last few inches I steadied them into their steps, and with a little sigh from the donkey they were lowered as gently as a feather falls.

When we left the Arsenale that evening, we walked most of the way backwards, so that, while *Tzu Hang* was still in sight, we could see her in her new rig, with her masts once more in place.

Every day the web of stays and shrouds grew about *Tzu Hang*'s masts, and every afternoon now the south wind blew strongly, splashing the wave tops over the mole behind which we sheltered. High above us *Esmeralda*'s rigging gave out a full-throated roar, and now *Tzu Hang* began to pipe a shrill accompaniment. We had set up the rigging using bulldog grips to hold the wire round the thimbles at the lower ends. Now we adjusted the rigging-screws, marked and cut the lower ends, and spliced in the thimbles, so that our stays and shrouds were all the right length, leaving just sufficient for stretch.

Every day I spliced and served, and as usual we had someone to help us. This time it was the crew of a disabled tug which lay alongside us. One of the seamen came from the Island of Chiloe, which breeds seamen for Chile, as the Hebrides or Shetlands do for Britain. He helped me with the splicing, but he didn't care for the stainless steel, and he preferred to cut rather than twist off his ends, so that when he was working, he started the splices and I finished them.

In the middle of October the ship which brought our stores from England arrived, and Beryl and I went down to the Company Offices only to find that two of the cases had been off-loaded in Valparaiso. Worse still the case that had arrived had been broken open and rifled, but we could not tell how much was lost until the other case arrived. We were spending so much in refitting *Tzu Hang* anyway, that for once we had ordered all that we really wanted for her, but up to now had managed to do without. It was a bitter blow, and we had little hope that the cases in Valparaiso would arrive intact. I arranged with the shipping company that when they arrived on the following boat, they would not be left for the night in lighters made fast to the quay. When the ship arrived we found them next day lying in the lighters, where they had spent the night. Both cases had been broken open and over a hundred pounds worth of stores had been stolen.

I do not know where the theft took place. It may not have taken place in Chile, but there is so much of it during the voyage, at any port of call, and even, it is said, before the start of a voyage, that the company with whom we were dealing seemed helpless and fatalistic about it. Perhaps it is one of those penalties that have to be accepted if one lives with the beauty of the Andes as a background.

But at least the sails, the rope, the compass, and some of the blocks had arrived, and there was nothing to stop us leaving, and if we needed something to help us recover from this blow, we soon had it. Captain Bonnafoss returned from leave. The same afternoon the mainsail arrived from *Esmeralda*, and as it was a calm afternoon we were able to bend it on and set it. It was a new sail, and now that we had altered it we were pleased to find that it fitted splendidly. We went over to thank Captain Bonnafoss.

'Is there anything else that I can do for you?' he asked.

Beryl never misses a chance. 'We need some rawhide strips,' she said, 'for lashing slides and hanks on to the luff-ropes. We got some kangaroo-hide in Australia and found that it was far better for seizing them on with than marline, and better than shackles, which we always used before for the mainsail slides. We can't find any rawhide here nearly strong enough.'

'They use sea lion hide here for lashing the yokes on to the horns of the oxen, I don't know whether that would do you?'

'We were given a sea lion skin, but it smelt simply awful, and it was so thick and hard that we couldn't cut it.'

'Well, leave it to me,' Captain Bonnafoss said, 'I'm sure that I can manage something.'

A day or two later he turned up on board *Tzu Hang* with some long thin strips of rawhide in his hand. 'Here you are,' he said. 'What do you think of these?' He handed us the strips and when we tested them we found that we could not break them.

'What are they?'

'Well I'll tell you,' he said, 'because you'll never guess. They are cut from the hide of a female celibate puma.'

I thought of the several months that we had spent in Talcahuano. I though of the kindness that we had met with, and of the frustrations too, of the achievements and the disappointments, the delays and the successes. Many of them we might have experienced in other parts of the world; but nowhere else, I thought, could we ever have been given rawhide made from the skin of a female celibate puma.

CHAPTER THIRTEEN

TO CORONEL AGAIN

ONE day after we were back in the water, we found the inner harbour full of fish-boats. The sardines had come in. The fish-boats were moving round in a circle as their crews cast their nets, and then drew them tight and hauled them in. After hauling their nets they went off full to the gunwales, with their pumps working hard and so low in the water that it looked as if they might sink before they had unloaded their catch. As soon as they were unloaded they came back for more. The hungry cormorants from Peru, who had been dying all along the shores during the winter, soon began to look fat and sleek again. Perhaps the sardines were a sign that summer had arrived, for the gardens in Concepcion were gay with flowers, and the boisterous south wind sent little white wavelets scurrying across the bay.

We walked along the beach to the Admiral's house for the last time, in places clambering over rocks on hand and footholds that we had come to know well, and we ate for the last time one of Señora Young's prodigious and famous teas.

'So you are really off at last,' the Admiral said, 'and you are going south, not true? I think that I should like to go with you.'

'He would too, but I say he is too old now,' said his Señora.

'Too old, nonsense. Too comfortable perhaps,' the Admiral bridled.

We had all the charts from the Golfo de Peñas to the south, by way of the Channels, and we spread them out on the floor to go through our route with the Admiral.

'But you are going in very far to the south,' he said, 'it is a great pity that you will miss this part from Ancud, in here, where it is a very different country.'

'The thing is,' I said, 'we want to get on now as it is already much later than we intended, and for most of the time in the Channels we can only travel by day, and what with finding our anchorages and making our moorings secure, and getting away in the morning, with only two of us we'll make very short runs. I doubt if we'll average more than thirty miles a day.'

'That's true,' he said, 'but I think that at least you should go in south of Chiloe here, by Guafo Island. It is such lovely country. You must remember that the longer you stay at sea, the more likely you are to meet with bad weather, not true? In the Channels it is all sheltered water, but it is getting a little late, and down south in the summer you have too much wind. Fewer gales you know, but it blows strongly in the Channels always, and at sea a gale is a gale, and it can blow just as hard in the summer as in the winter.'

'Still we should be able to get into the Golfo de Peñas without trouble.'

'I don't know. If you are thinking of going into the Golfo de Peñas, it can be very bad there, and difficult to see the mouths of the Channels. Perhaps it might be better to go in at Trinidad Channel, which is straight and easy to find, but no further south than that. If it is bad in the Golfo de Peñas, then you must go in here behind the peninsula Tres Montes, and wait.'

The Admiral knew the Channels well, and was a mine of information about them, and we learnt as much as we could.

It may seem a little foolhardy that the two of us should have undertaken this trip alone, after our previous warning, but then, before Clio was old enough to be a useful hand, the two of us had sailed *Tzu Hang* a long way. We were also certain that the accident that we had met with before was because we were running before a heavy gale, and that if we had followed our usual custom by lying a-hull it would never have happened, or at least in not such a violent manner, and we believed also that we had met an exceptional wave.

I have heard it said that there are no such things as exceptional waves, but I believe that it might also be said about the sea as about the weather, that the only thing constant about it is its inconstancy. Scan the horizon for a time during heavy weather and sooner or later some distant wave will hump up above its fellows and an underlying swell or a change in the wind may turn this wave into an exceptional and terrifying monster.

It was such a wave that Sir Ernest Shackleton met with during his open boat journey from Elephant Island, and I believe that we met another just at its most dangerous time and shape. With more experience I do not think these waves are so rare, especially in that particular piece of ocean, but perhaps it is exceptional that a yacht and such a wave should meet, and I'm sure that a small ship may go through many gales, even there, without meeting one.

At any rate, whatever sort of a wave had overtaken us, the result to *Tzu Hang* had made a deep impression on Beryl and me, and we both dreaded another big storm in those waters. It was this fear of another big storm that made us feel we must face the danger again, but we didn't speak about it to each other because we do not discuss our private fears, and to go and do something at our age because we were afraid of it seemed a little immature.

As far as I was concerned, to take the ship south and through the Straits of Magellan was all that I needed to get this feeling out of my system, and I didn't mind how soon it was before we got into the Channels, but Beryl wanted to get out to sea, well out, and to have her storm, which we were almost bound to have sooner or later, and then to run as quickly as possible through the Straits of Magellan, watch and watch if possible, until we reached the Atlantic.

For Beryl the Atlantic counted as home waters. She wasn't keen on the Channels as she had already made the trip in a steamer, and it had been wet and cold with poor visibility all the way. She wanted no fooling about with anchors and dinghies and lines to the trees, which would have been very tiring for the two of us, with more opportunity to get into difficulties than we would normally experience at sea.

We could make the Channels at the Golfo de Peñas, at Trinidad passage, or right into the Straits, where the lighthouse at Los Evangelistas, well out from the entrance, was a good landfall but where the average wind force at 7 a.m. was 5·7 Beaufort Scale. It would depend on how the ship was sailing, the weather, and how we felt about it when we got to sea. At any rate we both felt the same about the trip north and through the Panama Canal. We had made that decision some months ago. Now we thought that it was time to make our first move, and to take *Tzu Hang* to Coronel for an initial test, and to complete the odds and ends of fitting out there.

In order to fill up with water we went alongside *Esmeralda*, and she topped up our tanks with her hoses. Jim Byrne, who wanted to make the trip with us to Coronel, arrived on board with a duffel bag, in time to relay to the seamen at the water cock, on the other side of *Esmeralda*, the agonised shouts from below, as our tanks overflowed. Only two of the water tanks are filled by deck fillers. Captain Bonnafoss looked over the rail for a moment and called down to us to come on board for tea, and later Admiral Young arrived too, and we talked until it was time for dinner. The talk went round to heavy weather and to what was the best action for us to take during a storm.

'I know what I'm going to do next time,' I said, 'I'm going to have the father and mother of a sea-anchor made, and no more running.'

'But why do you want to use a sea-anchor?' asked Captain Bonnafoss. 'I don't believe,' he said, 'that the sort of sea-anchor you two could handle would ever hold a ship like yours up to the sea, except by the stern. She is bound to fall off by the bow, and then you would be opposing some resistance to the sea, and you would be in a far worse position than if you just took everything down and let yourself drift away from it, broadside on to the sea. We have had *Esmeralda* stopped in a gale, and lying broadside to the sea, and she drifted away sideways, her drift making the water smooth to windward, so that there is no danger from the waves.'

'Well, that's what we've always done before, but I don't know how it would be further south in those big seas. The smooth made by *Tzu Hang*'s drift is so small it has no effect on the big waves at all.'

'Just take it easy, take it easy,' said Captain Bonnafoss, 'take down all sail and wait for it to pass.' He was a big confident man, and he made us begin to feel that it was all quite easy after all. Admiral Young, in his gentle way, agreed, but we all knew that as long as he had some canvas left to spread, he would keep on going. 'You are really a little late for the Channels,' he said, 'and then if you have a gale outside, you must wait, not true? Do not try to make them if it is blowing hard.'

Next morning, long before the bugles had sounded on *Esmeralda* or *Latorre*, we cast off our lines and made for the narrow entrance to the docks. There wasn't a breath of wind and we motored quietly along outside the breakwater and up into the Boca Chica, but before we turned the end of the breakwater we gave old *La Fortuna* a wave.

It was full daylight by the time we were level with Admiral Young's house, and in spite of the early hour we could see a white sheet waving. We dipped our ensign and hoped that they could see. A small boat detached itself from the shore and we could hear the purr of an outboard engine. It was the Admiral and his daughter coming out to see us off in the smallest boat that could possibly hold an admiral and his daughter. They escorted us towards the mouth of the Boca Chica, and some porpoises came rolling alongside.

'That's the best possible luck,' the Admiral shouted. 'They only come inside for exceptional luck. Everything is going to be all right.' He turned his little boat round and waved goodbye.

When we got outside the Boca Chica, our old friend the fog rolled up and we beat away from the shore, in poor visibility and with a light wind from the south. The regular summer southerly swell was running, and Jim, who had been steering with a salty, weather-beaten look on his face, began to look green. The wind strengthened, and *Tzu Hang* began to pitch awkwardly into the sea. Beryl and I were very interested in her performance under her new rig. With the working staysail she seemed to go well enough, and also to balance well, but I didn't think that she was as fast. Beryl thought that there was so little difference that she couldn't notice it, and she accused me of thinking that she was slower because I expected her to be. She wasn't so fast, but she had never been a fast boat anyway, and it made little enough difference.

We were soon on the other tack, past Ramuncho Light on Punta Gualpen, the northern entrance to Arauco Bay, and the hills looked green now, which had looked so brown from the sea eight months ago; then we ran into smoother water as we came into the shelter of the bay. The Genoa has always been *Tzu Hang*'s best sail, and when we set it now, it pulled her along as before. As I stood in the bow against the pulpit rail and looked down at the forefoot hissing cleanly through the water, I didn't regret the vanished bowsprit, although bowsprits have all sorts of valuable uses, because *Tzu Hang* was sailing herself quite easily and without any fussing with the tiller, and that and the uncluttered foredeck and the ease in tacking were compensation enough. Jim began to feel better. A short time before he had had some trouble with an incipient appendix, but now he felt sure that even his appendix had gone over the side.

We tied up to the coal wharf at Coronel with two long warps to the wharf and a stern-line to a buoy, but the swell came roving in, and it was a most uncomfortable berth. Bob came on board next morning with three engineers, to check on anything that still needed doing, so that we could get off with the least possible delay. The spare generator had to be wired up, in order to be able to charge up the batteries with the shaft disconnected and the propeller free, and the lights had to be wired. The tiller was slightly crooked on the post so that the casting required fairing, and we were going to make a sea-anchor out of metal pipe and thin galvanised sheeting. Bob was quite oblivious of the motion below, but his engineers passed out one after the other, and I began to feel seasick myself.

We went ashore for lunch, and Bob's bright-eyed, sparkling wife, Lila, said to Beryl, 'And if there is anything you want, a bath or anything, you must come to me, Mijita, and I want you to stay with me; now hold my hand,' she said, 'I say it truly, but truly, I want you to stay with me, and we have, if you want a doctor, a very good young doctor at the coal-mine, very good-looking, and we have a very good and modern hospital too.'

'And we've got a very good cemetery just above,' said Bob. 'You can stay there too if you want to.'

A few days later, when we were almost ready to leave, Beryl felt suddenly ill when she turned in, and was sick during the night. I didn't realise how ill she was until the morning, when I saw that she wasn't absolutely conscious of what she was doing. I got the thermometer out of the medicine cupboard, but it was in a foreign scale, which meant nothing to me, except that it looked alarmingly high. I rowed ashore to ring up Bob, and Lila answered.

'But Mijito,' she said, 'that is terrible, isn't it? I mean a little higher and it is death. Now listen. You must bring her ashore to me at once. Bob will send you the launch, and you must take her to the other pier so that she hasn't to walk too much, and Bob will meet you with the car. Now I will arrange for the doctor.' Lila was just the person for an emergency.

Almost as soon as I was back the launch arrived, and Beryl got up from her bunk, but no sooner had she got to her feet than she fainted, clean out, to the cabin floor. When she came round we helped her up and loaded her on to the launch. She looked desperately ill, and I had to half carry her down the wharf. Bob was waiting for us with the car, and I saw from his face that he was shocked at her appearance, but she was soon in bed, with Lila, the gentlest of nurses to fuss over her. The young doctor tried every drug in the book but she reacted immediately to injections of emetine. She had had a virulent attack of dysentery, which had flared up suddenly, when her resistance was low from a cold.

In a few days she was on her feet again, and soon seemed to be quite recovered, but we put off the sailing for another week. I thought that if she didn't seem really well, when we got to sea, I would take her up north, but she knew what I was thinking, and said to me, 'If you think that you're going north after this, you can go by yourself, because I would regret it all my life.'

'Well, what will you do then if I go by myself?'

'Anyway,' she said, 'I'm not supposed to go into the tropics. They're bad for dysentery.'

The truth of the matter was that neither of us were thinking very rationally about this trip now. Getting away had been too much of a struggle, and Beryl regarded this illness as just another obstacle to be overcome, which made her all the more determined to go south, and I had a feeling, too, that to take the easier way would end in bad luck.

One day she said to Bob, 'You know, when I was ill and you met me on the wharf, you were thinking about that nasty crack of yours about the cemetery, weren't you?'

'By God, I was,' he said.

At the end of the week we could look around *Tzu Hang* and feel that she was really ready for the long passage, in better shape than she had ever been before. We had had a long piece of angle-iron, curved to fit the cracked deck-beam, made for us in the workshops. It was bolted on to the deck-beam, and the two ring-bolts, to which the twin forestays were fastened, were bolted through it. Two ring-nuts were screwed on to the lower end of these bolts, and wire leads led from these to two rigging-screws which were fastened to the iron floors of the ship. Whatever happened to the mainmast, the deck-beam couldn't be pulled up again now.

The height of the masts had been reduced, which was an improvement for the southern trip, and, as we had already discovered, there didn't seem to be a great difference in her sailing. The doghouse was lower, without the loss of any comfort, and it was more securely fastened than before, and so were our cabin skylights. The working sails were all new, or nearly new, and of terylene, as were the sheets and halliards; and the stays and shrouds, and the wire parts of the halliards, had all been renewed in stainless steel, except the lower shrouds, which were galvanised.

The sea-anchor, which was made out of light steel tubes, and thin galvanised iron sheets, set at right angles with a gap between, was stowed just behind the mast and in front of the dinghy, with its rope coiled inside it, with the thimble shackled on to the wire leads of the sea-anchor. It was all ready for use, except that it needed a spinnaker pole to float it, and was light and strong. Bob thought that it would stand up to any strain we could subject it to, but as we never used it, I cannot say how effective it would have been. The dinghy, lashed upside down on the deck, we had never been in.

Below decks *Tzu Hang* was the same as before except that we had taken one of the water tanks as an extra petrol tank. The planking that we had used for the masts and spars had all been replaced, and she looked snug and comfortable once more, with a brightly coloured Chilean rug on one of the bunks. In the main cabin two gaily painted little lifebelts, modelled out of wood, were hanging on each side on the bulkheads. They had been given us by one of the officers in the Arsenale, as a remembrance of our stay in Chile. The word 'Hang' was neatly painted on the top of the ring, and 'Talcahuano' underneath. They were the only lifebelts that we had.

One member of the crew had yet to join us. Pwe was still leading a luxurious life in the Avenida Pedro Valdivia. At night the ginger tom fought desperate battles on her behalf and by day, battle-scarred and exhausted, he slept in the garden, but he never won the least sign of approval from the lady who had brought such a turmoil into his life.

The three maids were there to see her off, when we took her away, hoping perhaps that she would be allowed to remain with them, for they were all very fond of her. After so much pampering and attention, we wondered how she would take to the ship again, and during the drive to Coronel, shut up in her basket, she screamed the whole way. She yelled even louder when we put her on the launch and the engine started, but the moment that she was on *Tzu Hang*, she sat down and purred and purred.

Beryl and I felt absurdly grateful to her, as if she had given us a present, she was so very pleased to be home.

Edward, who had driven the three of us back from Concepcion, had brought us a case of Pisco, and Molly Byrne now brought us a specially sweet and sticky cake for the voyage, and we had bought two even sweeter and stickier called *torta Doña Paulina*. They were supposed to last indefinitely, but they were so good that we were unable to test their capacity for endurance. They consisted of glutinous layers of something brown and unbelievably good. Last of all Marta arrived with a Christmas parcel done up in special wrappings, and with instructions that it should not be opened until Christmas Day.

We sailed on Monday, December 9, with a very light breeze from the south. We cast off the buoy, hoisted the Genoa, and slid quietly away. Then we went about, hoisted the main and mizzen, and sailed back past the end of the pier. A collier was coming in to load, and she discharged a lot of evil-smelling oil into the bay. We sailed sluggishly through it, and slowly turned our head for the entrance to Arauco Bay. We could see some people waving from the seafront by Bob's house, and then *Tzu Hang* began to quicken her pace, and we were off. It had been a long time.

CHAPTER FOURTEEN

NOT AGAIN!

We were off ... and yet, except for the first time that we set sail in *Tzu Hang*, I have rarely felt less confident at the start of a voyage. It was nothing to do with *Tzu Hang*, and a look round the decks was enough to convince anyone that she was in as good shape, or even better shape, than she had ever been before. Certainly there was less clutter about the decks, she was obviously going to be easier to handle, and there was no doubt about the strength of her masts—in spite of the knots—nor of her stays. The feeling was partly due to reaction after the long effort to get away, partly to worry about Beryl's recovery, and partly to a doubt of our own ability if it came to another struggle with those cold southern seas.

We were later than ever now, so we decided to go straight down to the Straits of Magellan. One of the factors in this decision was that we had had no confirmation that the two drums of gasoline that I had ordered had been delivered at Puerto Eden, half way down the Channels. I wished now that I had made arrangements direct with the Chilean Navy, who would have dropped them for me without any doubt.

The route south is against the prevailing southerly wind and the north-setting current, so that a sailing ship sails to the south-west, close-hauled until she gets down to the favourable westerly winds, and the westerly drift of the current. By the time the wind is fair for the Horn, or for the Straits of Magellan, and it is time to go on to the starboard tack, a ship may be 300 or 400 miles offshore, and I should say that a small yacht should be at least 200 miles otherwise it is getting too close to a lee shore.

For three days we pitched into the swell and made fair progress against wind and current. For some of the time the wind was in the south-west, so that, as close-hauled as we could sail, we didn't make much to the south. We didn't mind how far offshore we went as Beryl was feeling better every day, and we wanted to be sure that she was fit before we got out of the good weather. It took me a long time to find my sea-legs and I was gloomy and depressed. On the fourth night we were becalmed, and I couldn't sleep, and because I couldn't sleep was beset with morbid thoughts about the dangers of our landfall and the entry into the Straits.

'What on earth's wrong with you, you old mope?' Beryl asked me next morning.

'Good God,' I thought, 'how perfectly dreary I must have been!' and took a deep breath and shook off the depression, feeling ashamed and selfish that it should have been so obvious.

From then on, although we were idling so slowly down into the forties, about 300 miles offshore, I have never enjoyed a trip more. Every day Beryl looked better. She was delighted to be at sea again, and away from the worries of fitting-out. At breakfast she drank her second and even her third cup of coffee, buried in a book, sitting in the cook's chair with the cat on her lap, and knowing that she could take as long about it as she liked. At lunch she chumped up her raw onions, blissfully aware that there were only Pwe and I to complain, and I became a confirmed onion-eater in self-defence. We were near the track that we had sailed under jury, and marvelled at the runs that we had made with so little sail, for here we were with every stitch set and unable to equal them.

While we had had the wind the current had been against us, and now that we seemed to be out of the current, there was no wind. The glass climbed slowly up to 31·2 with a cloudless sky. We were really yachting, and Pwe, like us, spent much of the time on deck revelling in the sunshine. It was like being on leave during the war. We knew that somewhere in the south was hardship and danger, and that we had to go back into it, but for the time being we were making the best of this lazy weather, enjoying every minute of it but knowing that it had to come to an end soon.

At seven o'clock every evening I used to get the time signal from London on the B.B.C. news. At seven o'clock Edward would be turning on his radio in the Avenida Pedro Valdivia and Lydia we hoped would be bringing in his Pisco sour, or perhaps he had got into bad habits and was no longer drinking Pisco. We always thought of him when we got the time signal, but we decided not to broach the case of Pisco until Christmas Day.

We had told Clio that it would be two months at least before she might expect any news of us. If we were caught by a gale on our way in towards the Straits, or in case of bad visibility, it might be necessary for us to run further south for the Horn. We thought that two months should cover any eventuality, and didn't feel any necessity to press on now. Nor did *Tzu Hang*. She crept south, doing what Captain Bonnafoss had recommended and taking it easy. Slowly south she went, over a great rolling desert of a sea, with nothing to be seen over all its changing distances except a leisurely quartering albatross, appearing and disappearing over the blue dunes.

Eleven days had gone and we had had one short period only when the wind had got up to gale force. We lay a-hull for a short time, not because it was really necessary, but to reassure ourselves of *Tzu Hang*'s behaviour. Now, on December 21, there were signs that our honeymoon was over. During the night the glass fell quickly, and soon after midnight we reefed the mizzen and the main. Reefing was easy now, with the roller reefing, and we never hesitated to adjust the sail to the wind's force. But after reefing, the sail didn't seem to set quite so well as it had in the more laborious days, when we hauled down the reefing cringles and tied the reef points. The wind veered slowly until it was coming from the north-west. Our first depression, a small one, was on its way, but as we were down to 45° S. it was time to expect one.

At four in the morning we handed the mizzen, rolled down some more of the main, and set the small staysail, steering now because the wind was on our quarter on a southerly course. There was a fresh cold wind and breakfast tasted doubly good after the watch on deck. We steered all morning. By midday the wind was backing and we were able to set more sail and let *Tzu Hang* off on her own again. We had made 120 miles by noon, and most of them since midnight, so that at last she had been stepping out in her old style. But it was a grey miserable day, typical of the onset of another southern depression, and the glass rallied for a short time only and then continued to fall. From 31·2 inches, which had marked the long sunny windless high, it fell to 29·5 inches, and we were sailing south under the full main and the small jib only.

At nightfall on the 23rd the wind dropped altogether, but the glass was still falling, so we made all secure for a gale. It was the night of the new moon. 'If there is bad weather on the night of the new moon there will be bad weather every fourth day until the moon changes,' the Admiral had said to us, 'on the fifth and ninth day, and as she came in so she will go out. That is the Chilean saying.' I told him that I didn't think that the meteorologists would agree that bad weather had anything to do with the moon. 'I don't know about other parts of the world, but that's how it is in Chile; any fisherman will tell you, not true?'

By four o'clock in the morning it was blowing hard from the south-west. When we went on deck and checked the lashings and ties on the sails, the wind whipped our collars against our cheeks, a familiar cold wind which we had felt so often on the passage from Australia, so that I looked at the hatch, expecting to see John's burly figure coming up to lend a hand. Down below *Tzu Hang* felt safe and warm, and by the time it was over and she had ridden it out without any trouble, we felt confident that all we had to do, in much worse conditions, was to 'take it easy'. With reefed mainsail and the small staysail we made off for the south again; making five knots and rough going.

All across the Southern Ocean, especially during the latter part of our previous passage, depression had followed depression, with only occasionally a high. As each depression had passed, and the wind had swung to the south-west or south, with the sun breaking through clearing skies, the glass had shot up, and it had only started to fall again with the approach of another low, and the wind veering to the north. But now two depressions had passed, and yet the glass had scarcely halted for the change in the wind, and nothing seemed to stay its slow and ominous fall.

On the morning of December 24 the wind was round in the north again, and we decided to rig the twins. We handed all sail while we had breakfast, and then started to work, rigging the staysail booms with lifts and foreguys, so that when we wanted to take in sail, we need only let the halliards run, and then we could lash the sails to the booms before trying to bring them in. With this rig one of us could look after the sails, while the other watched the helm. As we worked, the wind swung to the west again, and we set the jib and sailed under it alone. In the afternoon we set the reefed mizzen, and later the Genoa, making some wonderful sailing all through a brilliant afternoon. We were joined by some porpoises, leaping and diving about our bow. They were white with black saddles and piggy pink faces which we had never seen before and altogether the most striking and charming porpoise visitors that we have ever had. We changed back to the jib for the night, with the wind veering once more to the north. It was Christmas Eve and a very solitary one. We thought of Clio in England.

Next morning we set the twins early, and hurried on to the south. We opened our Christmas parcels at breakfast and found Pisco and Vermouth and cigarettes and biscuits, a feast for the sailors. The glass continued to fall. The wind was soon blowing force 7 and strengthening. Somewhere to the north-west a dark monster was brooding, sending his messengers on before with the news of his coming, so that his shadow already seemed to brood over the sea, and the ragged clouds came flying, and the sea's long swell came rolling, to tell us that the danger which had threatened for several days was approaching now.

By midday the wind was blowing force 8. We drank Clio's health, and then Edward's, and Marta's. We finished everyone else off in a single bumper toast, and ate the second *torta Doña Paulina* in a finger-sucking orgy. We ate sitting in the doghouse below the half-open hatch, with all the washboards in place. Above the noise of *Tzu Hang* and the hum in the rigging came the rising and angry talk of the waves.

In the afternoon *Tzu Hang*'s progress was beginning to be too exciting. To stand in her bow in front of the twin staysails, with one hand on the forestay, and to look down into the valley of the sea below, was to realise all the thrill of topping a steeple-chase jump and seeing a sudden drop on the other side. There was something reckless about the feel of her movement, as if she would run whatever the weather, flinging herself gamely forward on each succeeding crest. She was exultant, not overburdened, it was akin to the feel of a good horse, who will not tire and, if the rider is able, will not fall. The riders in this case had had enough of it before nightfall, and we decided to shorten sail.

We hanked the storm-jib to the forestay, and rove the sheets and then put a tie on the sail while we turned our attention to the staysails. They were beginning to flutter at their peaks again, and it was time to take them down. With *Tzu Hang* stern on to the seas we let the halliards go together, the staysails ran down the stays, and in a moment we had tied them on the booms. *Tzu Hang* slowed, and she began to swing slowly. Beryl walked aft to the tiller, slipping the snap-hook of her life-line along the rail, until she could reach the shrouds, when she jumped into the cockpit and corrected the helm, while I set the jib. With the jib up *Tzu Hang* began to sail again, so that we were able to lash the helm, and she continued to sail with the wind and sea on her quarter. Together we brought the booms inboard, unbent the staysails, and secured the booms along the rails.

Beryl was wearing her black oilskin trousers, sea-boots, and her yellow oilskin jumper and hood. Her knife and spike were hanging on a cord from her waist, where her life-line was also knotted. She opened the spike and undid the shackle at the tack of the sail. Then she bundled up the sail in her usual vigorous manner and pushed it up to the hatch. Perhaps with a Pisco-induced sentimentality, I thought of her as I had heard someone describe her in Chile, '*Qué buena compañera*' … There was a flavour of buccaneers and swords about the Spanish words.

We went below and *Tzu Hang* ran on into the night under her little storm-jib, heading south with the wind and sea on her quarter, and it was still safe to leave her unattended. We didn't think that we would be able to let her run for long, as the glass was down to 29·2 inches when we turned in.

Through the dark restless hours she reeled on, while the mugs on their hooks, the stoves in their gimbals, and the shadows from the cabin lamp, swung in unison to the quick lurches. There was little sleep for either of us, and we were glad when with daylight the rising note of the wind, the almost incessant noise of spray on the deck, and the deeper sound of the seas, told us that it was time to stop. We got on deck to find that the spindrift was lifting and that wide crests were breaking all round. *Tzu Hang* had done well to keep on going through the night. Beryl took the helm while I pulled down the jib and put it away. Then I joined her in the cockpit. As a wave passed we put the helm down, and she swung slowly. The next wave caught us beam on, but without breaking and nothing came on board, and then she swung slowly up towards the wind, but fell away again into the trough, and began to drift sideways to the wind and sea. We lashed the helm down so that if she fell away and began to sail again, it would bring her up. The water boiled up from underneath her keel as she drifted and made little swirls and eddies along the weather side of the ship, but it made little difference to the water to windward and in a very few yards the smooth trail of her sideways drift had disappeared. As I went below I looked at the glass and saw that it was 28·8 inches. When I tapped it, it moved downwards again.

By ten o'clock the gale was at its height, and the glass was down to 28.6. There it stayed. The sea had taken on its whitish look again, all streaked and furrowed with foam, the low raddled sky was grey, and the wide white tops came roaring up on the spume ridden wind. 'Don't let the *tigrés* get you,' they had said to us when we left Talcahuano, and here they were after us in earnest, flinging their raging crests far ahead of them, and striving for a kill.

We either lay on our bunks and read or watched the seas through the doghouse windows. Sometimes we could see a shaggy monster raise his head above the others, and sometimes a wave would seem to break all down its front, a rolling cascading mass of white foam, pouring down the whole surface of the wave like an avalanche down a mountainside. There was no point in speculating what would happen to us if one of them hit us, in fact the whole business of watching the seas seemed to us unprofitable. The most terrifying toppling masses of water as often as not passed us without even a slap, but the wind would bellow as we rose on a wave, and *Tzu Hang* would heel away from it. Then we would hear the wave grumbling and growling away, spreading an ever-widening swath of foam behind, and as we sank into the hollow the noise in the rigging fell.

'What do you think?' I said to Beryl. 'Do you think that we should try and put the sea-anchor out?'

'I don't know,' she said, 'I think that it's a bit late. She seems to be doing all right, doesn't she?'

'The glass seems to have stopped falling now, and she's done all right so far, and we don't really know how the sea-anchor is going to work, so we'll leave her as she is.'

I did not think of using oil, and although we had some spare engine oil we had no oil-bags. I decided not to use the sea-anchor because I believed that with all the sea-room we needed we would do best lying a-hull. I knew that there was danger, but I thought that the sea-anchor would only succeed in holding the bow half up to the sea, offering an ineffectual resistance, which would be worse than drifting away. Moreover, although we had had the opportunity, we hadn't yet tried out the sea-anchor, and now it looked as if it would be dangerous work getting it out. We were doing what we had done successfully in other gales, but never in such bad conditions as these.

'Do you think that we're imagining that it's worse than it really is?' Beryl asked.

'I don't know about imagining. I know it's quite bad enough and I'll be damn glad when it's over.'

'So shall I,' she said with feeling.

We lay down on our bunks again, Beryl in the forecabin and I in the main, and both on the port side, the side of the greatest heel, but we kept our boots and oilskin trousers on. Sometimes, when *Tzu Hang* heeled very quickly and steeply, or when we heard a deep rumbling roar approaching, we clutched the side of our bunks tense and anxious, and held our breath, and when it was over we looked at each other with a rueful grin. The cat went from one to the other to be petted, pricking her ears and crouching at the more alarming sounds, but on the whole less anxious than we were.

At four o'clock I thought that I'd make some tea. It was summer and for ten hours now it had been blowing a full gale, so I thought that the change must come soon, now that the glass had steadied. When the glass began to rise the wind would still blow for a few hours, but this must be the worst of it now. Almost as I thought this, *Tzu Hang* heeled steeply over, heeled over desperately into a raging blackness, and everything within me seemed to rebel against this fate. All my mind was saying, 'Oh no, not again! Not again!'

Again the water burst violently into the ship, and again I found myself struggling under water in total darkness, and hit on the head, battered and torn in a kind of mob violence, and wondering when *Tzu Hang* would struggle up. I could not tell what was happening to me, but I knew all the time what was happening to

CAUGHT BY ...

... A BREAKING CREST

the ship. I felt her heavy and deep as the keel came over, and felt her wrench herself from the spars deep below her. I heard the noise of their breaking, and saw the light again from the port skylight, as it spun over my head. I found myself struggling to my feet knee-deep in water, and saw Beryl doing the same in the forecabin. I scrambled aft. The doghouse was still there, badly stove-in on the lee side, and the hatch was gone. When I looked out, I saw that the mainmast had gone at the deck, and the mizzen at the lower cross-trees. The broken spars were lying on the weather side of the ship.

CLEAN OVER

UPRIGHT AGAIN, WITH WRECKAGE TO WINDWARD

'It's all the same again,' I said to Beryl, who was just behind me, and as I said it a sluice of water poured into the doghouse. I climbed up on deck to look at the ruin, and heard Beryl say, 'I'll get the jib.'

The ship was drifting away from the broken tangle of spars fast enough to prevent them smashing into her when they rode up on the waves, so they were not endangering her. The first thing to do seemed to be to get the doghouse covered and secured. The whole top had cracked off and shifted forward, but it was still held by the after corner posts, which had pulled away from their corners. The cockpit also had been burst open, and one of the skylights in the main cabin was torn off. 'By God, we've done it once, and we'll do it again!' I said and at once felt stupid, as my detached and cynical self noted the heroics, and noted also that there was no one to hear, and that Beryl was already doing something about ensuring that we did 'do it again'. I jumped down to her, and we pulled the No. 1 jib into the doghouse, and found some rope to make it secure. For hours we had been waiting under the threat of the storm. Now the crisis had arrived and we had something to do. Mercifully it looked as if we might be able to deal with it, and there was a feeling of relief that we were not, as far as we could see, in such desperate straits as in the first accident—a feeling of relief, too, that at last we were at grips with the situation that had haunted our imagination for so long, and troubled our minds until we had come south to meet it and do our best.

During my short visit to the deck I had felt the bitter wind whipping through my wet jersey, and, remembering the cold that I had suffered before, I fished up an oilskin coat and put it on. I found another for Beryl, and held it out for her, saying to her, in the most incongruous surroundings, 'Do put a coat on, dear. It's so cold outside.' Both of us had bleeding heads, but otherwise seemed all right.

We pulled the Genoa on to the deck, and with some difficulty, owing to the force of the wind, folded it roughly over the doghouse. We worked on our knees, but at times were buffeted with such a weight of spray that we found it difficult to keep on the deck. After getting the sail in place, we lashed it round and round, and then over and over, from ring-bolt to ring-bolt, so that both the sail and the doghouse were held firmly down. Then we climbed down through the skylight and started to bale in the same way as we had baled before, with a plastic bucket. We had to bale in order to find the hammer and some nails, for all the ship's stores had again emptied out of their lockers, and lay in wild confusion in the water below. By half-past eight we were able to explore the bilge and found the hammer and some 2-inch copper nails and with these and a jib we climbed once more out of the skylight to deal with the cockpit.

If anything, the conditions on deck were worse than before, and no sooner had we reached the weather side of the cockpit than we were swept again by a mass of white water. We grabbed for the remaining shrouds, and when the water had cleared, we thought that we'd lost the hammer, but found it again wedged under the broken rail. Another wave swept us, so that we were separated from each other, and the whole ship seemed to be under water, and this time the hammer was gone. Beryl climbed down through the skylight again and brought up the wooden mallet, and while I stretched the sail over the boards we had nailed across the cockpit, she nailed it down. We were continually left gasping and sodden, and felt an unreality about the situation, as if we were acting a tableau of two people clinging to the shrouds of a wave-swept wreck, in an old-fashioned picture. While I stretched the sail and held the battens in place, I kept an eye to weather, ready to shout a warning to Beryl to catch hold of the shrouds.

Nothing is more exasperating than watching a left-handed woman with numbed fingers trying to hammer 2-inch copper nails into a teak deck. It would be bad under the best of conditions, but now it had all the ingredients of a nightmare. The nails folded over one after the other, and when I could get the opportunity I grabbed the mallet, only to find that I made a worse job of it than she did. Beryl pounced on the mallet again and finished the job. By the time we had nailed some battens along the side of the doghouse, and covered the skylight, it was getting dark, and for the last twenty minutes we had had no great amount of water on the deck. The wind was beginning to ease. As I closed the forehatch, and followed Beryl aft, I had a vivid feeling that there was someone behind me, and turned round to see, but of course there was no one there.

We pulled the spare primus out of the cupboard in the fore-peak and filled it, and we made something hot. Beryl called for Pwe and she answered from aft, and we found her somewhere in John's berth. She was very disgusted and wet too, but she was not suffering from shock. We sorted out the bunkboards in the forecabin, and were able to find a comparatively dry mattress and we all lay down together for warmth.

As we lay, cold and unable to sleep, Beryl kept saying, 'At any rate we have got plenty of time. There is no need to go rushing about and getting exhausted. We'll just do a little and then we'll have a rest.' She was thinking that there was no John, and that we might get over-tired, and perhaps sick. Much later on, after we had slept a little, the full enormity of the situation burst upon me. Here we were, almost a year after the first accident, in very nearly the same place, all our work gone, all our plans brought to nothing again, and Clio still in England and we the wrong side of South America. I gave a quite involuntary and mournful groan which I can still hear with shame. It made Beryl reach for my hand and ask quickly what was the matter.

'Oh dear,' I said, 'it's the thought of going back.'

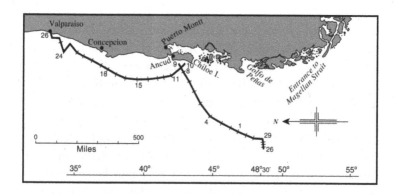

CHAPTER FIFTEEN

THERE'S A WIND FROM THE SOUTH

THERE was nothing else that we could do. We would have to go back, and it was time to start thinking how. We had not had a sight for two days, and while we lay on the bunk, I tried to figure out how far we had come, and how far to the east we had been driven during the storm. About 48° 30′ S., I thought we were, and perhaps 300 miles offshore. That was the worst of our predicament. We were farther north than the first time that we were disabled, but much closer to the coast. Making allowances for the westerly drift while we rigged our jurymast, I thought that there might be little room to spare by the time we got into the southerly winds and the north-going current which would carry us up the coast to safety.

We got up and made breakfast, and after the miserable night that we had spent, we felt better as we thought of what we had to do. First of all, again, we had to make the ship secure, and directly we had finished breakfast, we went on deck to plan the repairs.

The broken spars were still attached to their rigging and floating to weather, and now that the wind was down and *Tzu Hang* no longer drifting away as fast as before, they came riding up on the swell looking as if they were going to smash into her side. The danger was much reduced as each mast was broken in three pieces, but we released some rigging-screws and the wreckage rode further away. The lee rigging-screws of the main and middle shroud, each calculated to take a seven-ton breaking strain, had sheared; the lee rigging-screws were the ones to weather when *Tzu Hang* was upside down, or the upper ones as she rolled upright again. The masts had to go anyway, and I felt glad that the screws had broken, as long as the hull was undamaged. Something had to go under those stresses, and anything was preferable to the hull. The rest of the damage on deck could be easily seen. The pulpit was smashed down in the centre, the weather rail stanchions were bent all over the place, and the capping broken. The unused dinghy was gone, and the ring-bolts in the deck to which it had been lashed by terylene rope were bent as if the rope had been wire cable. The sea-anchor and its hawser were gone, and 18 feet of rail and the patent log had been torn away on the lee side. Both boom gallows were gone, but the mizzen boom with its sail attached drooped wearily on to the deck, where we had lashed it by its sheet the day before.

The rest of the damage could be seen better from below. There was little left of the port side, the lee side of the doghouse. Splintered pieces of the side, with the torn and twisted copper framing of the windows attached, had been pushed inwards into the house, and all the perspex had been shattered. The top of the doghouse had been broken off, the hatch was gone, and the starboard windows cracked in several places. The engine had emptied its oil out of the filler cap, and filled up again with sea water, and the dip-stick had fallen out and through the hatch, or so we suppose, because it was nowhere on the ship, and was never found again. One of the deck-beams aft, near the mizzenmast, was broken, although we didn't find it out until some time later, and the fore-and-aft beams at the bottom of the cockpit to which its fibre-glassed sides had been screwed were broken outwards, towards the sides of the ship, so that there were gaps between the sides and the floor.

In the main cabin most of the damage had been done by the big five-burner, cast-iron enamelled stove. The bolts which secured it must have been rusted, because it cut loose, and now lay broken in several pieces on the cabin floor. It had left some horrible scars on the deckhead, and I had a black eye which I supposed was something to do with it. It had also smashed the cabin table, which slid up on a brass pole to the deckhead; it had bent the pole and torn it from its fastenings. Though I had been taking part in this merry-go-round, I had come out of it with very little hurt.

Although everything was out of the drawers in the forecabin, it is on a higher level than the main, and we were spared the awful invasion of water. Apart from the bilges and the floor it was comparatively dry. A minor but annoying disaster in the after part of the ship was that a can of paint had lost its lid and emptied its contents into the bilge, where it mixed with some broken bottles of Pisco. There was a winy smell about the bilge, like the wine-shop in the corner on Pedro Valdivia, where we used to wait for the buses to take us up the road.

The radio set, the barometer, and the chronometer were all completely out of action, and the two coastal charts which I had had on the chart table had vanished, so that in respect of aids to navigation, we were much worse off than before, but Beryl had been trying to rate her wristwatch before the accident, so that we could expect to be reasonably close to the time. The rating had been upset by a convulsive change which occurred in the watch just before Christmas, but we decided to ignore that spasm.

So much for the tale of the damage. It took us three days to get the ship more or less to rights, and on the third day we hoisted our first sail. But the first job that we had to do after pumping out the ship was to fix the doghouse and cockpit properly. We pumped out quite a lot of water, and it began to look as if there was a leak somewhere. *Tzu Hang* had never leaked before.

We pulled away the splintered side of the doghouse and screwed three boards on to the corner posts to make a new side. Beryl had taken over the job of ship's carpenter from John, and I could see that she was determined to do a job that her instructor would be proud of, if ever he came to hear of it. 'Just bash it on here,' I said, but no, it had to be drilled and screwed. We replaced the No. 1 jib with the Genoa, carefully folded, and lashed it all down again, and we took the boards which had once been the sides of our jurymast, and fastened them over the sail along the deck at the sides of the doghouse. We covered the deck well with caulking compound before doing this and the result was a reasonably leak-proof cover. In order to nail the copper nails with the wooden mallet, we drilled holes in the deck, and used the old screw holes in the boards. After the doghouse was finished, we fixed up the cockpit properly, and also the skylight. Then we were reasonably satisfied that we could stand another gale.

In the evening Beryl showed me a rash that was coming out on her hands and wrists.

'What on earth's causing that?' I asked.

'I don't know. Perhaps it's something to do with salt water.'

'It looks to me like some sort of allergy.'

'An allergy to being turned over,' she said. 'I've had too much of it anyway.'

She couldn't sleep owing to the irritation, and next day was covered with it. We thought that it must be something to do with the drugs that she had taken for her dysentery, and it made her very miserable for a day or two.

For the first day or two also, we both felt very tired. I suppose that it was a reaction to the violent strife of the storm. We took many rests in our bunks in the forecabin, which was reasonably comfortable, judged by the standards which might be expected in yachts which had been turned over in a South Pacific gale. One person who approved most heartily of these rests was Pwe. Although she had recovered very quickly, she objected most strongly to being below while we worked on deck, and always sat up in the forepeak, as close to the forehatch as she could scramble. By the end of the third day the ship was beginning to get into shape again. Our spirits rose and we began to feel some exhilaration in the adventure. We thought that it would be a good show if the two ancient mariners pulled it off by themselves and brought the ship back to port again. For the first day or two I had a strong feeling that a third person was present, a feeling that there was someone still on deck with me when Beryl was below, and sometimes that there were two people below.

'I expect it's just that the last time we were like this we had John with us,' Beryl said, when I told her about it. This was a very reasonable explanation. But it is a feeling, a vivid sensation of someone else being present, that has been experienced and written about by mountaineers and sailors, under similar conditions of stress.

With the pumps working again, we found that it only took a few minutes to get the ship dry, provided that we pumped three or four times a day, and we were able to trace the leak to one of the few butts in *Tzu Hang*'s planking, but as far as we could see the fastenings there were still intact. We found out long afterwards that the caulking had come out from between these two butts. As soon as we had located the cause and extent of the leak it gave us no more anxiety.

The first sail that we hoisted was a mizzen-staysail and we hoisted it by throwing a wire halliard over the remaining mizzen cross-tree. The stump of the mizzenmast was a forlorn looking sight, with jagged splinters showing above the cross-tree fitting. Only half the cross-tree remained, and about 10 feet of mast-track, torn from the upper part of the mast, still whipping about as the ship rolled. Next morning both it and the wooden half of the cross-tree were gone. Using the bronze base of the cross-tree arms, which were angled slightly upwards, as a sheave, we hoisted the staysail upside down, the tack at the mast-head, a sheet to the clew, and the head lashed to the weather rail in front of the mainmast stump. I can't say that *Tzu Hang* really began sailing. She was hove to, making some headway, and drifting slowly to leeward, but it steadied her movement and was an advance in the right direction, and I started to think about the new sail-plan.

We still had the red storm-jib, that had done us so well on our previous trip under jury, and we had the little raffee, the gallant little warhorse, which we had never used before the first accident, and which had then towed us up to the north, so impatient of control and so violent in its tantrums. We also had the two staysails which we had taken off on Christmas Day and stowed below, the mizzen which had been on the boom and wasn't lost in the accident, and one of the headsails which we had not used for covering the damage.

Before we left Talcahuano we had dismantled the jurymast, the hollow 20-foot mast, and now we had used most of the pieces that we had saved in nailing down the sail coverings to the deck. We had also kept the spar which John had cut and glued with so much labour, and so much smoke, from the butt of the mainmast, and we had not been able to bring ourselves to throw away the original jurymast that he had made by splicing the two spinnaker poles together. It was a question of sentiment. The spar had been lashed along the rail on the foredeck and was still intact. The spliced spinnaker poles had been smashed in two, but by one of those freakish tricks that the sea seems to play in these turmoils, half had remained on deck. Of the two spinnaker poles in use, which were clipped on to the main shrouds, and along the top of the life-line to a stanchion on each side of the ship, only half of one remained, still clipped on to a shroud, which trailed over the side into the water. With the mizzen boom as a mast and the old jury spar as a topmast, we would be able to make a 16-foot mast, and we could use the broken spinnaker pole as a mizzen boom.

I saw that only the centre part of the mainmast now remained in the sea to weather. The other parts and the mizzen had broken away. Beryl was below resting and recovering from her allergy, and the sea was going down. I thought that at least I might be able to save some of the rigging that was still attached to this part of the mast. I hauled the broken piece in; it was heavy, and as it came near it swooped on *Tzu Hang*'s side, giving her a wicked bang, which brought poor Beryl flying to the hatch in great distress at the idea of *Tzu Hang* suffering further injury. We decided to let it go, and it floated away under the solemn inspection of two albatrosses.

Next day Beryl was nearly recovered, and we set up the new mainmast. We cut the mizzen boom from the gooseneck with a hacksaw, leaving about half an inch of the bronze shaft of the fitting to stand in a wooden step, which we nailed to the deck. Using two jib bridles to make four stays, with stainless steel wire portions and terylene rope purchases, we set it up without any difficulty, with spare shrouds as forestay and backstay, and lengths of chain and rigging-screws to adjust the length. When we had finished, the boom was as secure a little foremast as we could wish. Next we hoisted John's spar as a topmast, and as the band on the spar was not in the centre, we could hoist it short end or long end up, according to the amount of sail that we wished to carry, and on several occasions we set it in the reefed position. On January 30, four days after being disabled, we were sailing again, and the wind was in the west.

Tzu Hang sailed splendidly up to the north-east, sometimes with her mizzen, mizzen-staysail, main and raffee, showing quite an imposing display of canvas, and sometimes with only the raffee straining like a little demon at its sheets, but usually with the raffee and a staysail hoisted upside down as the main. Her runs climbed into the seventies, but we couldn't pretend that we could get to weather, and hoped for southerly winds before we got to the coast. Our course, as we plotted it with the help of Beryl's wristwatch, looked as if we would make the coast in the region of Chiloe, unless we found the south wind. If we were forced into the Channels we would be in dire need of the engine. As soon as we were sailing, I set to work to try and make it go. I suppose that a real mechanic would have coaxed that engine somehow so that it would have started before the feeble life in the battery died. One battery had lost all its acid, and the other had fallen out of its box and broken one of its leads, but it still had a slight kick in it. I pumped the salt water out of the engine and filled it up again with oil, and cleaned and dried the distributor and points. We heated the sparking plugs on the stove, cleaned out the carburettor, and did everything that

UNDER THE JURY

we could think of. While Beryl pressed the starter button, I knelt down and wound the left-handed starting handle, the lowest reach being somewhere down in the bilge. This position of kneeling, with my head almost level with the cabin floor, in fact prostrating myself before the engine, gives me a feeling of defeat before I've started, and I know that inevitably I'm going to bark my knuckles or hit my head with the end of the starting handle in a gesture of abasement. Fortunately it only happens when the battery is dead. Now the salt-water-soaked leads gave too many outlets for the feeble current, and under these conditions it was impossible to get a spark under compression. After a long struggle we gave it up. We would have to trust to our jury sails to bring us in.

Where we had found a fresh southerly wind and fine weather on the first trip under jury, we now had dull overcast skies, frequent rain squalls, and the wind obstinately in the north-west or west, so that we found ourselves steadily closing the coast of Chiloe, and on the 8th, making a guess at the error in Beryl's wristwatch, I thought that we must be only eighty-six miles offshore. It was an anxious time.

The Island of Chiloe is about 100 miles long, stretching between latitudes 41° 50′ and 42° 30′ S., where the coast of Chile first begins to break up under the continuous assault of the sea, driven by the westerly winds of the forties. There is no anchorage along all its western coast. North of Chiloe is the Golfo Coronados which leads into the Golfo Ancud, and to Puerto Montt, the first port north of Magallanes. If we could get into Puerto Montt, it was possible that some time or other we could get *Tzu Hang* shipped out. At any rate we could get temporary repairs done there, good enough to sail out, but without an engine it was impossible to get up the Chacao Narrows between the north coast of Chiloe Island and the mainland, a long narrow passage with swirling dangerous tides.

In the Golfo Coronados and on the north shore of Chiloe Island is the port of Ancud, but the same tide runs fast past the entrance, and we would be extremely lucky if ever we could manoeuvre *Tzu Hang* into shelter. It looked as if we would have to rely on the faint hope of finding a fishboat outside to take us in tow. South of Chiloe the Channels would be entered by a passage past Guafo Island, but the coast there was only sparsely populated and there was little hope of assistance. The tides run strongly, and we had no dinghy. Though we could almost certainly save ourselves if we got in, we didn't think that we would be able to save *Tzu Hang*, and even if we did, we didn't know how on earth we would recover her. We didn't want anything to do with any of this coast here. We wanted a south wind to take us offshore and into the sun and smoother seas, so that we could approach or hold off the land as we wished, but if the south wind wasn't coming, we had to make up our minds and go boldly through with it, because waiting about in our present position could only bring disaster. We decided to try for Ancud.

That night the wind blew hard from the north-west, and there was every sign that the glass was falling, although we had no glass to see. We got a fix on the 9th: it was obvious that we couldn't possibly make Ancud, even if the wind went as far as the west, and we couldn't tell how deep this depression was. If we held on much longer, even if we hove to for long, we would be soon on a lee shore, something to be respected in the forties, even in summer, by an able yacht—something to be dreaded by a cripple. In spite of this we took down our sail for a few hours, and let a warp go over the side to check our drift a little. In the evening the wind was lighter, but still north of west, and with heavy hearts we turned about, set our sail again, and made for the south, hoping to squeeze a little further offshore, and if the worst came to the worst to get into the Channels by Guafo Island.

Except for the night of the second smash it was the worst night that I have ever spent, because of the miserable feeling that after all the effort we were going the wrong way again. Beryl turned in and slept peacefully. I felt quite angry that she could do so, and after one of my numerous trips to the hatch to listen anxiously for breakers, I heard her snore. The worst of it was not knowing exactly where we were, and not having a chart of the coast. All I had was a page from the American chart catalogue, but after Beryl's snore I thought that if she could sleep, damn it, I could too. I turned in, worried and indignant, and did in fact go to sleep.

I woke up soon afterwards, feeling that something wonderful had happened. Not knowing quite what it was, I lay for a moment, joy and relief spreading over me, as if I had dreamed a great happiness. A cold wind was blowing down through the hatch. It was something new. I scrambled to my feet and looked out—looked out to strange stars in a topsy-turvy sky, to small sails aback, and a cold wind from the south. I slipped back into the cabin and bent over Beryl where she was still sleeping, and shook her gently: 'There's a wind from the south,' I said.

In the next thirty-two hours we sailed ninety miles to the northwest, and from then on the south wind stayed with us. It had been late in coming, and had come just in time. But now it stayed with us, and we knew that in all probability it would bring us safely home.

From then on the whole feel of the voyage altered. We were in high spirits, with Cape Horn and the Straits of Magellan well out of our systems, perhaps for good. One of the reasons for this holiday feeling was that this time we were insured. We had had to pay a high premium, but we had done it because all the rocks in all the anchorages of the Channels are not yet charted, and as a sort of mumbo-jumbo to insure that there would be no need to be insured. We didn't think that a second accident like the first could possibly happen, and if it did we didn't think it likely that we would be lucky enough to survive a second time, so we had arranged that no claim would be made if we were lost. It is possible that the underwriters had the same ideas.

Now, when we looked over the damage, and saw that we needed almost the same repairs, we knew what it would cost. On the first occasion we had had many facilities allowed by the Navy free, facilities such as the use of power tools and sheds, and a lot of friendly assistance for nothing; all the work and materials at the coal-mine had been at cost price and we had done most of the work on the yacht ourselves. Now that we were 'an insurance job' it was going to be a very different tale, and at a conservative estimate it was going to cost twice as much as before. We knew that the cheapest way to repair *Tzu Hang* was to ship her to England. We wanted to reach a port from where she could be shipped, and where there was a Lloyds surveyor who knew what he was talking about when it came to comparing relative costs. We thought that we would only find that in Valparaiso, 240 miles north of Talcahuano. We also thought the many people who had shown us so much kindness in Talcahuano and Concepcion might well regard such an early return with horror. So, full of confidence now, off we set for the north. But we would have been very glad to know the right time.

Tzu Hang sailed steadily up to the north. On January 18 we figured that we were 100 miles west of Arauco Bay, and on the 22nd that we were 200 miles on our way and only thirty miles offshore. This put us on the shipping lane from Valparaiso to the south and we kept night watches again. One evening Beryl thought that she saw land, and although we could make out a high dark outline through the lower haze, which didn't change, it was impossible to say whether it was the high Andes or dark distant cloud, or the lower foothills and that we were reasonably close inshore.

Next morning was dull and overcast, and there was no sign of land at all as we waddled slowly northwards. Beryl and I were fit and rested; we read and practised Spanish together, and the cat seemed content for the voyage to go on indefinitely as long as she had plenty of attention and food. About ten o'clock when we were both on deck hoping for a glimpse of the sun through the clouds, I saw smoke ahead, and at the same time the ripple faded from the sea, and our sails hung limp and flapped as we rolled.

The smoke grew until a mast and funnel showed over the horizon, and then a high bow, and a white wave curling, which splashed up as the little ship pitched into the gentle southerly swell. She was steaming fast on a course that would take her past us a mile away. As she drew near she swung towards us, black smoke pouring from her funnel, and rolling worse than *Tzu Hang*. My memory flicked back to a similar ship and a similar sea, which had also turned towards us like this, but that was off the west coast of Vancouver Island, and I saw that this one too was a whaler, and we could make out the look-out on the mast and the harpoon-gun in the bow.

As the whaler came up to us, its engines slowed, the bow wave died, and it steered past us about 100 yards away. The captain came out from the wheelhouse, the cook from the galley. All the crew lined the rail, and a wild gang of pirates they looked. They stared at us and we at them, waiting for the engines to go astern and the ship to stop. The captain stepped into the chart room and came out again with a large megaphone. We thought that we would be able to get our position all right now, but we were wrong. '*Buen viaje*,' he shouted, '*Buen viaje*,' and the water boiled under the whaler's stem, and she leaped ahead, with all the crew waving, leaving us dumbfounded.

'What on earth?' said Beryl. 'Why didn't you shout to him?'

'But I thought he was going to stop. What in hell does he think we are, the *Tahiti Nui*?'

We made very little progress, but we did get a position line in the afternoon. As far as we could make out we were only a few miles offshore, but it was hazy weather, and we doubted if we could see the shore even if our position was correct. We kept watch again that night but saw no light and no ship. Next day we were becalmed again, and just as we were taking our midday sight, we saw smoke approaching.

'This time I'm going to yell blue murder,' I said. While the ship was approaching, I worked out our position, and found it a few miles west of San Antonio. Again the ship, another whaler, altered course and steamed up to us, and as it closed we shouted and beckoned to it. This time it stopped and swung round like a polo pony, and lay broadside on close to us. A magnificent figure, a prince of buccaneers in a black coat, who looked as if he had personally pulled his ship to a halt and twisted it round, stared down at us from the bridge.

'*¡Buenos días!*' we shouted across to each other.

'*¿Qué distancia desde San Antonio?*' I asked. The captain dived into the wheelhouse and reappeared almost immediately with his megaphone: '*Setenta y cinco millas,*' he said, and I expected to see the sound waves rumple the oily swell between us.

'Seventy-five miles,' Beryl and I looked at each other in surprise.

'*Nuestro cronometer es quebrado,*' I explained.

'*Conforme.*'

'*E el motor también.*'

'*Conforme. ¿Qué otras cosas?*'

'*Nada. Muchas gracias.*'

'*Conforme. Hasta la vista.*'

The whaler shuddered, and the throb of her propeller rang through our own hull as she began to shoulder her way through the swell with the captain standing on the bridge, his arm extended in a dramatic gesture of farewell. Even at that range his personality seemed to dwarf the ship and his crew, and we felt sorry for any whales he sighted. When I told him about the engine being out of action, I had half hoped that he might send an engineer on board, loaded with batteries, to put it right, but we had never asked for help at sea, and we weren't going to now. But the whaler swung round, making a smooth slick as she turned, and came up alongside again. It looked as if the captain had just understood some of my Spanish, and had come back to hear some more.

'Do you think he's going to do something about the engine?' Beryl asked. We waited expectantly as the captain leant over with his megaphone.

'*¿Son ustedes alemanes ó ingleses?*' he asked.

'*Somos ingleses,*' Beryl shouted.

'*Ha. Bueno. ¡Hasta luego Señora! ¡Buen viaje!*' and he swept off his cap and bowed, as his ship swirled away again. There was no doubt about it. We were back, or almost back, in Chile, with its gallantry and its improbabilities.

'Seventy-five miles,' Beryl said. 'We needn't have kept watch for the last two nights after all.' I thought that perhaps we hadn't been quite so close to the coast of Chiloe as I had supposed at the time, and I need not have got into such a sweat about it. We lay becalmed for the rest of the day. After midnight a small breeze came from the south, and we sailed due east in order to make our landfall well to the south of Valparaiso and with a wide margin for the northward set of the current.

Next morning, January 25, we had a fresh southerly wind, which freshened all day until it was blowing strongly, and *Tzu Hang*, in spite of her jury-rig, seemed to be racing in for the shore. In the afternoon we could see a headland, which we thought must be Punta San Domingo, but we held on in a wind force 6 to 7, until we could see some houses and a low beach. Then we took down our sails and waited for the lights to show. As darkness fell the whole seafront lit up with innumerable lights, and wherever we looked, over the rough sea, lights seemed to be either flashing or occulting.

'Flashing one in three, isn't it?' Beryl asked.

'Yes, but look, there's the light. It's occulting every five. Good Lord, isn't that one of the Valparaiso lights?'

'It can't be. Let's count again,' Beryl said.

'Right. There … two, three, four, five, six, seven … what the hell?'

'Try again.'

'There … two, three … it's moving. It must be a fishboat.'

'No, there's the light. I saw it flashing. There, farther round.' Beryl pointed. And it was. San Antonio, and for the first time since we were disabled a month before we knew exactly where we were.

As soon as we knew where we were we made sail, sailing north a mile or two offshore. At first we continued to make good time, but gradually the wind fell and the sea calmed. We had no doubt now of our ability to make port, but there was an anticipatory thrill about the idea of doing so, and we enjoyed every moment of our night watches, seeing sometimes the headlights of a car on the roads ashore, sometimes the lights of a fishboat, and once a big cargo ship going south, and always the faint glow in the sky from the lights of Valparaiso ahead.

In the morning we were closing the jagged rocks of Curaumilla Point, and the craggy little island of Los Lobos, and we thought of the Seal Rocks that we had set off from over a year before. Another ten miles, idling slowly down the coast, and Valparaiso Bay, with its ships at anchor in the roads, began to open out before us. The wind carried us in in the early afternoon until we were nearing the breakwater, but there we were in the lee of the high ground, and the south wind failed. We had finished up with the best run of all, under jury-rig.

Only a short distance ahead we could see the land breeze ruffling the water, blowing right into the inner harbour. We got out the dinghy oars and started to paddle *Tzu Hang* towards it, but a man in a small harbour launch came up and offered his assistance.

'We haven't got any money,' we said, as we had no *pesos* left on board.

'But of course not; no matter. Where do you want to go?'

We had already noticed *Esmeralda*'s tall masts above the break-water. 'Take us to *Esmeralda*,' we said. As soon as we arrived alongside, some seamen ran to take our lines, and to make us fast alongside, and the harbour launch went off with a delighted owner clasping an unexpected bottle of Pisco. Then there were baths and supper on the *Esmeralda*, and the kindest of welcomes, and no one to say, 'I told you so,' but only, 'Well done!'

A few days later I had a letter from a friend in Santiago; 'I don't know what would have happened to the British reputation in Chile,' he said, 'if it hadn't been for you two...'

'By George,' I said to Beryl, 'that's jolly good of him. Listen to this,' and I read it out to her. But when I turned over the page, the letter went on, 'reputation for eccentricity, I mean.'

Two months later *Tzu Hang* came up into London River on the deck of a freighter, and was off-loaded at the West India Dock. From there she sailed under her own power, for the big ship's engineers had been busy on her engine, to Burnham on Crouch in one day. During the passage we rigged the little jurymast and sail, which had helped us back to Valparaiso, so that it brought her home in the end; but before we left London, in fact as soon as we arrived, Beryl and I hurried off to Lewes to see Clio.

A green bus drew up at the corner where we were waiting and, as a tall girl stepped out, I felt Beryl start forward and heard her say, 'Good heavens, she hasn't changed at all!' and later, during one of those meals which astound parents all over the world, Clio said,

'Are you going to have another shot?'

'No,' I said, 'I think that once is enough,' and I looked across at Beryl.

'And twice is really too much,' she went on, and suddenly I felt that all that had mattered so much to us, during the last few months, had slipped into its proper place in the past, into the perspective of a life.

CHAPTER SIXTEEN

EPILOGUE

GIVE a man—or a girl for that matter—a horse he can ride, and sooner or later he, or she, will want to ride further and faster and to jump higher. Let a man climb one mountain and he must find another until he seeks the snows. It is the same with a ship. 'Though never of great worship myself,' said Sir Dinadan, 'ever have I loved men of great worship.' It is this love of men of great worship that sends us off, humbly and often ineffectually, in their footsteps or in the vanished furrows of their keels.

Capes and seas, like mountains, 'are there' to round and to cross; and adventure, even when not in search of knowledge and without scientific aim, is good for its own sake. Only when it involves other people unwittingly or involuntarily in one's own distress is it bad. But even in this respect there may be another point of view, as Jim Byrne pointed out to us in Chile. 'I think you ought to let people rescue you,' he said. 'It gives them a tremendous lift. The rescuer is always the hell of a chap, and the rescued gets slapped down. It's jolly decent of a chap to let himself be rescued.'

Beryl and I don't agree with Jim. When a small yacht sets out on a long journey, it must be entirely self-reliant. There will be no help near when trouble strikes. If the ship is out only for adventure and sport it has no right to expect help, and it is just as well if it has no means of asking for it.

I have called this story *Once is Enough*, but once is never really enough in any worthwhile sport. The mountaineer coming down from a high mountain may look over his shoulder and say, 'Well that's that. Never again!' But no sooner is he down at the base camp than he is wondering whether another route will 'go'. The same with a yacht and Cape Horn. Once, or twice, may be enough for Beryl and me and *Tzu Hang*, but certain it is that other yachts will still try it. Some will be successful, and some like us will fail. It isn't a trip to be undertaken lightly, however good the ship, and the story of our passage and the experience of what might happen to a yacht like *Tzu Hang* in those big seas, may add its little molecule to the mountains of knowledge of ships and the sea.

We asked too much of *Tzu Hang*, and she gave us of her best. On each occasion she brought us safely home, which is all that a good ship can do. Now—bless her—fully equipped again, she is lying at anchor in Mulroy Bay, and Pwe, grown stout and placid in quarantine, and the dog, Poopa, are messmates once more. Sometimes a letter comes from John, still on his way across the seas in *Trekka*, and often we think of the days together in *Tzu Hang*, and then we wonder, on those two days of her trial, how we could have helped her more.

On the first occasion if we had had a sea-anchor out on the end of our rope, a really good sea-anchor, with wire strops to a thimble, and shackled to a swivel fastened to another thimble in the end of the rope, and if we had used oil at the same time—a constant flow from a special tank—to smooth the sea in our wake, we might have avoided the somersault, which I am quite certain we made.

The other time, if somehow or other we could have made *Tzu Hang* lie four points off the wind, rather than broadside to the sea, we might have escaped damage again. Perhaps if we had sent a very small and very strong riding sail from the mizzen, as trawlers do, and if we had streamed a sea-anchor from the bow, we might have done so.

If I was to take a small ship in another attempt to round Cape Horn, and I mean round Cape Horn on the old sailing-ship route, I would have one built. She would have broader beam than *Tzu Hang* and shallower draught, and then perhaps she would not be bowled over, if due to some misadventure I was forced to lie a-hull. She would be a ketch again, with very much shorter masts of almost equal height, and the only deckhouse would be amidships over a self-draining cockpit, so that I would avoid gaping holes in the deck. I would hope that her hull design would let her ride to a sea-anchor by the bow, with a very small and stout riding sail, or safely by the stem, and I should have a built in tank of oil, and most important of all I should want Beryl. Unfortunately I don't think that this dream ship would be much good anywhere else.

As a result of it all I think this: there are gales and seas which a good ship, a yacht, will come through whether she lies a-hull, heaves to, or runs before; and there are gales and seas, particularly in the higher latitudes, which a ship may sometimes meet with, which she will be lucky to survive whatever she does. Man does his best, but in the end something else intervenes. It may be the Pilot of the Pinta, who sometimes, for no accountable reason, brings ships home, and sometimes, for no accountable reason, lets them go.

MANAGEMENT IN HEAVY WEATHER

It is strange, but true, in the high southern latitudes, where seas can be 50 feet high and 2,000 feet long, they roll forward in endless procession with occasionally one sea of abnormal size towering above the others, its approach visible for a considerable distance.

Captain William H. S. Jones, *The Cape Horn Breed.*

WHEN wind and sea become too strong for a small ship, there are two alternative actions that she can take. She must stop or she must run. If by running she is closing a lee shore or going in the wrong direction, it is better that she should stop, and in order to do this she can either heave to, or lie to a sea-anchor, or lie a-hull.

Some yachts heave to with a headsail aback, and with reefed main or a mizzen. Some yachts will heave to under the reefed main alone, or under a trysail alone, but however they do it, heaving to implies stopping under sail. In point of fact a ship hove to is not actually stopped; she is almost certain to be fore-reaching slowly, and drifting to leeward, so that her actual course moves slowly at right angles to wind and sea.

When seas are very big and winds exceptional there are special dangers in heaving to. The ship will head up towards the wind and fall away, and as she heads up the sail will shake so violently that it tends to tear itself to pieces, or to shake the mast out of the ship, and if it is not doing this the ship tends to lie between five and six points, or more off the wind, and is in danger of being hove down by the more violent gusts, and is also in danger of taking a breaking crest into her sail, with a weight of water which will bear her masts down into the sea.

When a ship, instead of heaving to, lies to a sea-anchor by the bows, there are also special dangers. The object is to lie with all sail down bows on to the wind and sea, and if a ship will assume a position not more than four or five points to the sea, that is taking the waves from head on to diagonally on her bow, she should be safe. There will be a great strain on her rudder as she drifts and sometimes is hurled backwards, and there is a great strain on the sea-anchor and its tackle. This must be as strong as it can be, with wire strops leading to a thimble and the thimble shackled to another thimble in the end of the hawser. The inboard end of the hawser must in its turn be spliced to a thimble, and shackled to the anchor chain, and it is advisable to have a swivel between the sea-anchor and the end of the hawser.

A canoe will lie to a sea-anchor, a ship's lifeboat will lie to a sea-anchor, and a small yacht may lie to a sea-anchor if she uses one big enough to hold her, but a yacht like *Tzu Hang* with the lighter draught of her bow and the deeper draught of her keel, with her high sheer and her foremast and rigging ahead of the centre of lateral resistance of the hull, cannot lie to a sea-anchor without some other assistance. She drags the sea-anchor round until she assumes a position little better than at right angles to the wind and sea; then she is in a worse position than if she had no sea-anchor at all, because like a pier or breakwater she is opposing some resistance to the sea, and as she is almost broadside on, she is liable to suffer damage.

It may be that if she is a yawl or a ketch a very small and tough riding sail could be set, as trawlers do, which would hold her up to the anchor and that a terylene sail, stronger than canvas for equal weight, and less liable to rot, would be the best. For this particular purpose it must be a special sail that can be set up taut and rigid. If she will then lie bow on to the sea, this is the safest course.

When a ship lies a-hull she is opposing the sea only with the weight of her hull and the drag of her keel; and it is possible that a light displacement yacht, steadied by a long warp streamed from the bow and stern in a loop, may even be picked up by broken water and carried sideways, without being rolled over. This happened recently to John Guzzwell in *Trekka*, when caught in a cyclonic storm off the coast of Queensland. But it is impossible to believe that a hawser streamed like this could have much effect on the equilibrium of a much heavier yacht.

A yacht of larger displacement and deeper draught is rolling to leeward as the first slope of the wave lifts her, a roll increased again as the wind catches her spars and rigging as they lift over the top of the waves. If on top of this she is hit by a breaking crest of many tons weight and is knocked to leeward by this rapidly moving water, while her keel is held in comparatively still water, she will be rolled on to her beam ends, and once her masts go into the water and the breaking sea gets under her keel, she is bound to go over.

When a ship drifts to leeward, as the water boils up under her keel, it leaves a smooth slick to weather. This slick, it is sometimes suggested, eases the sea to weather, but in fact it is only visible in a moderate gale, and in a strong gale it has not the slightest effect on the sea, only being visible for a few feet from the ship's side. With a big ship it is probably a different story.

When a yacht is lying a-hull she will usually fall off and try to sail on account of the pressure of the wind in her masts; with the helm lashed down, she will come up towards the wind, lose what little way she has, and fall off again. The result is a speed of about half a knot at right angles to the wind and drifting away with it, in a diagonal course to leeward. This forward speed has absolutely no bearing on the safety of the ship, except that it seems that it would be impossible—I have never tried it—to remain within the protection of one's oil, if oil is being used.

So many yachts—including *Tzu Hang*—have lain a-hull and come through gales safely, that it has come to be regarded, although only in recent years, as a seamanlike thing to do. Now I believe that it is the most dangerous course to take in exceptionally heavy seas. There is only one thing to be said for it: it is far better to be rolled over than turned stem over bow, if you want to talk about it afterwards.

If a yacht can lie bow on to the sea, as I have already said, I believe that she will be taking the safest course, but if she can't do this she will have to turn her stem to the sea, using every means available to check her way. I will not use the word 'run' because of the danger that it brings with it and which is described in detail below.

In the latitudes of *Tzu Hang*'s course from Australia, between 47° and 53° S., only the southern end of South America intervenes to break the swing of the seas as, driven by almost continuous westerly winds, they heave their way round the world. In a westerly gale when the wind can swing quickly from the north-west to the south-west, a hazardous irregular sea will build up on top of this permanent swell; more dangerous in the comparatively restricted

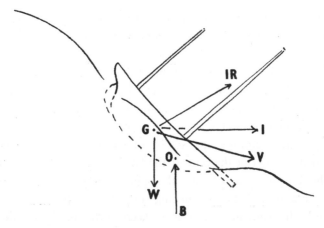

area south of Cape Horn, but dangerous enough for a small ship even in these latitudes. If she can be kept stern on to the sea a good yacht will run on straight and true in no particular danger, even though a breaking crest may very occasionally foam over the stern so that she seems to be running in a welter of white water. It is the abnormal wave, described in the quotation at the head of this Appendix, that brings disaster.

Soon after the accident I had a letter from Nevil Shute— amongst his many interests he is also a yachtsman—and the following description of what might happen to a yacht overtaken by an exceptional sea while running seemed to fit *Tzu Hang*'s case as exactly as if he had been there to see. I kept the letter and give the description now almost as it came to me.

As a wave of exceptional form races up from aft, the first slope of the wave will lift a yacht's stem so that she is well down by the bow. In this attitude the centre of buoyancy is probably somewhere about where it is shown in the diagram—marked 'O'. The centre of gravity will be about where it is shown, marked 'G' in the diagram. The forces of gravity acting through the centre of gravity and the forces of buoyancy acting through the centre of buoyancy therefore act as a righting couple, and if the ship was motionless she would be in no danger.

When a ship is running, even under bare poles, she may have considerable forward motion, and as the bow goes down the centre of gravity of the ship is still trying to go forward. This gives rise to a horizontal force on the centre of gravity, marked 'I' for inertia in the diagram, and it is opposed by a force exerted by the resistance of the water at the bow. If the angle of the boat was such that her bow went under water, the opposing force would be very near the bow, and the overturning couple would be large. This is one of the seamanlike reasons for keeping the speed low when running under bare poles.

There is, however, another force—marked 'IR' in the diagram—acting through the centre of gravity. If the stem is still going down there will be an inertia force acting through the centre of gravity forwards, rotating with 'O' as its centre. This force might be weakening as the boat assumes the position shown, but it could be strong. These two forces, 'I' and 'IR' when combined as vectors with the gravity force 'W' acting through the centre of gravity, produce a resultant force on the centre of gravity, marked 'V'. So long as this force passes below 'O' the ship is in stable equilibrium and the various couples are tending to right her, but once 'V' passes above 'O' they are tending to overturn her, and this could happen very quickly.

The forward speed has a great effect on this tendency, as without it 'I' would not exist and 'IR' would be unlikely to be serious, but once the forces begin to exert their influences as shown in the diagram, the bow tends to go still further down, until the ship turns stem over bow in an inverted position.

She is unlikely to come down in this position owing to the

weight of her keel, which will tend to roll her as soon as it gets clear of the water, and she will then begin to fall over until she comes down on her beam ends. The masts will be under water—and if she hasn't done so before—this violent roll will carry them away, and when she appears on the surface again she will be headed into the wind, facing in the opposite direction.

He went on to point out that a suitable sea-anchor would exert a very strong righting moment on the ship if she got into this unfortunate position, and suggested that the dinghy might be used, which I describe later on.

It is obvious that in order to avoid this danger of tripping over the bow, way must be taken off the ship. We have tried streaming a long rope in a bight from the stern, but the base of the bight is so narrow that it is ineffective. Even sixty fathoms of 3-inch rope proved ineffective, and when a breaking crest came up it carried the rope forward with it, halving its effective length.

A sea-anchor would have to be the type already described—the R.N.L.I. pattern made by Ratsey and Lapthorne is probably the best—or the dinghy might be used. In order to do this it would have to be slung in a strong rope net like a cargo net, fitted to its hull, with rope pendants leading from the edges of the net like parachute line to a single fitting, which would be shackled to the hawser thimble. In the days of nylon and terylene the net and pendants would not have to be too heavy and could be easily removed and stowed.

If a boat is going to lie by the stern to a sea-anchor, it is almost certain that, whatever her design, she will take some broken water over it. Her doghouse should be designed to withstand this, sloped both forward and aft, and her cockpit should be amidships. With this sort of arrangement she would be less liable to damage if heavily pooped.

In the end, however, it will not be any one aspect of design or action by the crew that will preserve a yacht in such severe conditions, but rather the sum of them all, and the use of oil will also play its part.

I cannot say that I have ever used oil in earnest, and the only time that I have experimented by using an oil-bag during a storm, we drifted diagonally away leaving a thin iridescent line on the surface; it afforded us no protection at all. Oil will not alter the shape of a sea, but it will smooth a breaking crest. It seems that to be used effectually it must be available in sufficient quantities and it must be easy of access. Few small yachts are equipped to use oil in any quantity, and I have little faith in small oil-bags in very heavy seas. A special tank, if there is room, is probably the best answer, with a lead through the hull, regulated by a sea-cock.

By the time we think of using oil it is probably needed badly, but there is little point in using it unless there is enough to have an effect on the sea, or unless the ship is able to remain within its protection.

POSTSCRIPT

SINCE I wrote this book I have had a number of letters—mostly from well-informed sources—on the reasons for *Tzu Hang*'s two mishaps, and the steps that we might have taken to prevent them. All those who have spoken and written to me, who have had practical experience of the seas in those southern latitudes, or who have made the sea and waves and the shape of a ship their study, have agreed that a ship of *Tzu Hang*'s size would need luck as well as seamanship to come through. Particularly the old, and some not so old, salts who have sailed round Cape Horn have wagged their heads and said, 'You should never have been there anyway; your ship was too small for those seas.'

This was already my opinion, but two letters helped to strengthen it. Both these letters suggested that, although the explanation and diagram of *Tzu Hang*'s overturning was correct to a certain extent, the major cause was probably due to the orbital velocity of a big wave. I had never heard of this theory which is that, although the mass of water in a seaway, seen as a whole, is static, each particle of water moves in an orbit round the place which it would occupy at rest. If we were to throw some rubbish overboard so that it represents a particle of water on the surface, we would see it drawn back towards the approaching swell, lifted up, carried forward, and dumped in approximately its original position again; seen from the side it would trace an orbit against the background of sea and sky.

The important thing is the speed at which the water moves in this orbit, and for a 40-foot wave with a ten second period the speed is approximately seven knots. With seven knots on the top of the wave with the wind, and seven knots against the wind at the bottom, a 40-foot ship on the point of a 40-foot wave is subjected roughly to a seven knot push one way at her stern and a seven knot push the other way at her bow, a formidable overturning couple. A longer ship is already overcoming the push at her bow by the time her stern is subjected to the maximum thrust. The answer seems to be to keep 40-foot ships out of 40-foot seas, but if forced to run before them to tow long enough lines so that there is an effective drag in spite of the forward movement of the water on the crest and lack of a swell.

Tzu Hang, Paris, March 1960

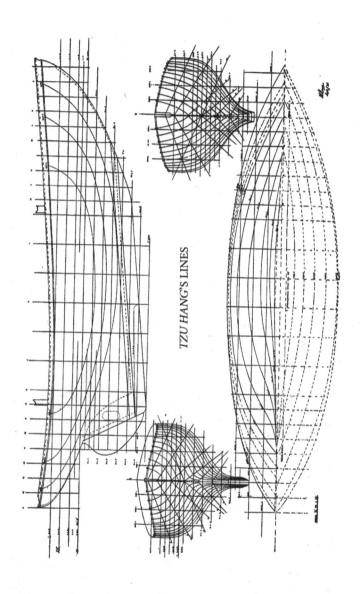

TZU HANG'S LINES